Services Offer
Complete Self-Assessment Guide

C000157520

The guidance in this Self-Assessment is based ⌐⌐ ⌐⌐ ⌐⌐
practices and standards in business process architecture, design and
quality management. The guidance is also based on the professional
judgment of the individual collaborators listed in the Acknowledgments.

Notice of rights

Trademarks

Table of Contents

About The Art of Service

The Art of Service, Business Process Architects since 2000, is dedicated to helping stakeholders achieve excellence.

Defining, designing, creating, and implementing a process to solve a stakeholders challenge or meet an objective is the most valuable role… In EVERY group, company, organization and department.

Unless you're talking a one-time, single-use project, there should be a process. Whether that process is managed and implemented by humans, AI, or a combination of the two, it needs to be designed by someone with a complex enough perspective to ask the right questions.

Someone capable of asking the right questions and step back and say, 'What are we really trying to accomplish here? And is there a different way to look at it?'

With The Art of Service's Standard Requirements Self-Assessments, we empower people who can do just that — whether their title is marketer, entrepreneur, manager, salesperson, consultant, Business Process Manager, executive assistant, IT Manager, CIO etc... —they are the people who rule the future. They are people who watch the process as it happens, and ask the right questions to make the process work better.

Contact us when you need any support with this Self-Assessment and any help with templates, blue-prints and examples of standard documents you might need:

http://theartofservice.com
service@theartofservice.com

Acknowledgments

This checklist was developed under the auspices of The Art of Service, chaired by Gerardus Blokdyk.

Representatives from several client companies participated in the preparation of this Self-Assessment.

In addition, we are thankful for the design and printing services provided.

Included Resources - how to access

Included with your purchase of the book is the Services Offer Self-Assessment Spreadsheet Dashboard which contains all questions and Self-Assessment areas and Self-Assessment auto-generates insights, graphs, and project RACI planning - all with examples to get you started right away.

How? Simply send an email to
access@theartofservice.com
with this books' title in the subject to get the Services Offer Self Assessment Tool right away.

You will receive the following contents with New and Updated specific criteria:

· The latest quick edition of the book in PDF

· The latest complete edition of the book in PDF, which criteria correspond to the criteria in...

· The Self-Assessment Excel Dashboard, and...

· Example pre-filled Self-Assessment Excel Dashboard to get familiar with results generation

· In-depth specific Checklists covering the topic

· Project management checklists and templates to assist with implementation

INCLUDES LIFETIME SELF ASSESSMENT UPDATES

Every self assessment comes with Lifetime Updates and Lifetime Free Updated Books. Lifetime Updates is an industry-first feature which allows you to receive verified self assessment updates, ensuring you always have the most accurate information at your fingertips.

Get it now– you will be glad you did - do it now, before you forget.

Send an email to **access@theartofservice.com** with this books' title in the subject to get the Services Offer Self Assessment Tool right away.

Your feedback is invaluable to us

If you recently bought this book, we would love to hear from you! You can do this by writing a review on amazon (or the online store where you purchased this book) about your last purchase! As part of our continual service improvement process, we love to hear real client experiences and feedback.

How does it work?
To post a review on Amazon, just log in to your account and click on the Create Your Own Review button (under Customer Reviews) of the relevant product page. You can find examples of product reviews in Amazon. If you purchased from another online store, simply follow their procedures.

What happens when I submit my review?
Once you have submitted your review, send us an email at review@theartofservice.com with the link to your review so we can properly thank you for your feedback.

Purpose of this Self-Assessment

This Self-Assessment has been developed to improve understanding of the requirements and elements of Services Offer, based on best practices and standards in business process architecture, design and quality management.

It is designed to allow for a rapid Self-Assessment to determine how closely existing management practices and procedures correspond to the elements of the Self-Assessment.

The criteria of requirements and elements of Services Offer have been rephrased in the format of a Self-Assessment questionnaire, with a seven-criterion scoring system, as explained in this document.

In this format, even with limited background knowledge of

Services Offer, a manager can quickly review existing operations to determine how they measure up to the standards. This in turn can serve as the starting point of a 'gap analysis' to identify management tools or system elements that might usefully be implemented in the organization to help improve overall performance.

How to use the Self-Assessment

On the following pages are a series of questions to identify to what extent your Services Offer initiative is complete in comparison to the requirements set in standards.

To facilitate answering the questions, there is a space in front of each question to enter a score on a scale of '1' to '5'.

1 Strongly Disagree

2 Disagree

3 Neutral

4 Agree

5 Strongly Agree

Read the question and rate it with the following in front of mind:

'In my belief, the answer to this question is clearly defined'.

There are two ways in which you can choose to interpret this statement;
  1. how aware are you that the answer to the question is clearly defined
  2. for more in-depth analysis you can choose to gather

evidence and confirm the answer to the question. This obviously will take more time, most Self-Assessment users opt for the first way to interpret the question and dig deeper later on based on the outcome of the overall Self-Assessment.

A score of '1' would mean that the answer is not clear at all, where a '5' would mean the answer is crystal clear and defined. Leave emtpy when the question is not applicable or you don't want to answer it, you can skip it without affecting your score. Write your score in the space provided.

After you have responded to all the appropriate statements in each section, compute your average score for that section, using the formula provided, and round to the nearest tenth. Then transfer to the corresponding spoke in the Services Offer Scorecard on the second next page of the Self-Assessment.

Your completed Services Offer Scorecard will give you a clear presentation of which Services Offer areas need attention.

Services Offer
Scorecard Example

Example of how the finalized Scorecard can look like:

Services Offer Scorecard

Your Scores:

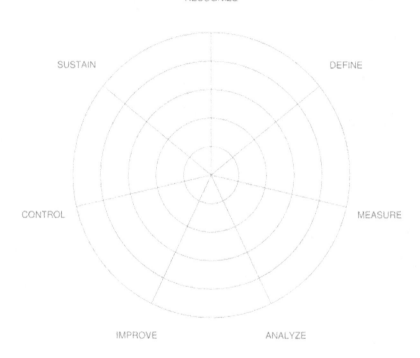

BEGINNING OF THE SELF-ASSESSMENT:

CRITERION #1: RECOGNIZE

INTENT: Be aware of the need for change. Recognize that there is an unfavorable variation, problem or symptom.

In my belief, the answer to this question is clearly defined:

5 Strongly Agree

4 Agree

3 Neutral

2 Disagree

1 Strongly Disagree

1. How does it fit into your organizational needs and tasks?
<--- Score

2. What Services Offer coordination do you need?
<--- Score

3. Are losses recognized in a timely manner?
<--- Score

4. Who needs budgets?

<--- Score

5. What should be considered when identifying available resources, constraints, and deadlines?

<--- Score

6. How many trainings, in total, are needed?

<--- Score

7. How do you assess your Services Offer workforce capability and capacity needs, including skills, competencies, and staffing levels?

<--- Score

8. Who needs to know?

<--- Score

9. Which information does the Services Offer business case need to include?

<--- Score

10. Who defines the rules in relation to any given issue?

<--- Score

11. How do you take a forward-looking perspective in identifying Services Offer research related to market response and models?

<--- Score

12. What needs to be done?

<--- Score

13. How are training requirements identified?

<--- Score

14. Will Services Offer deliverables need to be tested and, if so, by whom?
<--- Score

15. Is it needed?
<--- Score

16. What vendors make products that address the Services Offer needs?
<--- Score

17. Think about the people you identified for your Services Offer project and the project responsibilities you would assign to them, what kind of training do you think they would need to perform these responsibilities effectively?
<--- Score

18. What information do users need?
<--- Score

19. What does Services Offer success mean to the stakeholders?
<--- Score

20. What do employees need in the short term?
<--- Score

21. Are problem definition and motivation clearly presented?
<--- Score

22. Are there regulatory / compliance issues?
<--- Score

23. What resources or support might you need?
<--- Score

24. Is it clear when you think of the day ahead of you what activities and tasks you need to complete?
<--- Score

25. What else needs to be measured?
<--- Score

26. How much are sponsors, customers, partners, stakeholders involved in Services Offer? In other words, what are the risks, if Services Offer does not deliver successfully?
<--- Score

27. What is the extent or complexity of the Services Offer problem?
<--- Score

28. What are your needs in relation to Services Offer skills, labor, equipment, and markets?
<--- Score

29. Will new equipment/products be required to facilitate Services Offer delivery, for example is new software needed?
<--- Score

30. Does the problem have ethical dimensions?
<--- Score

31. When a Services Offer manager recognizes a problem, what options are available?
<--- Score

32. Are controls defined to recognize and contain problems?
<--- Score

33. Are you dealing with any of the same issues today as yesterday? What can you do about this?
<--- Score

34. Do you have/need 24-hour access to key personnel?
<--- Score

35. What Services Offer problem should be solved?
<--- Score

36. What would happen if Services Offer weren't done?
<--- Score

37. Will a response program recognize when a crisis occurs and provide some level of response?
<--- Score

38. Where do you need to exercise leadership?
<--- Score

39. What are the expected benefits of Services Offer to the stakeholder?
<--- Score

40. What needs to stay?
<--- Score

41. How do you identify and anticipate how requirements and changing expectations will

differ across customers, customer groups, and market segments and across the customer life cycle?
<--- Score

42. How can auditing be a preventative security measure?
<--- Score

43. What prevents you from making the changes you know will make you a more effective Services Offer leader?
<--- Score

44. Do you need different information or graphics?
<--- Score

45. Are employees recognized for desired behaviors?
<--- Score

46. What are the timeframes required to resolve each of the issues/problems?
<--- Score

47. Do you recognize Services Offer achievements?
<--- Score

48. Consider your own Services Offer project, what types of organizational problems do you think might be causing or affecting your problem, based on the work done so far?
<--- Score

49. Who needs to know about Services Offer?
<--- Score

50. Who should resolve the Services Offer issues?
<--- Score

51. Looking at each person individually – does every one have the qualities which are needed to work in this group?
<--- Score

52. What training and capacity building actions are needed to implement proposed reforms?
<--- Score

53. What Services Offer events should you attend?
<--- Score

54. What Services Offer capabilities do you need?
<--- Score

55. Would you recognize a threat from the inside?
<--- Score

56. Does Services Offer create potential expectations in other areas that need to be recognized and considered?
<--- Score

57. Which needs are not included or involved?
<--- Score

58. Whom do you really need or want to serve?
<--- Score

59. To what extent does each concerned units management team recognize Services Offer as an effective investment?
<--- Score

60. What extra resources will you need?
<--- Score

61. Who are your key stakeholders who need to sign off?
<--- Score

62. Are there any specific expectations or concerns about the Services Offer team, Services Offer itself?
<--- Score

63. How are you going to measure success?
<--- Score

64. Who else hopes to benefit from it?
<--- Score

65. What creative shifts do you need to take?
<--- Score

66. Are employees recognized or rewarded for performance that demonstrates the highest levels of integrity?
<--- Score

67. Are there Services Offer problems defined?
<--- Score

68. Are there any revenue recognition issues?
<--- Score

69. What are the minority interests and what amount of minority interests can be recognized?
<--- Score

70. Who needs what information?
<--- Score

71. Does your organization need more Services Offer education?
<--- Score

72. Can management personnel recognize the monetary benefit of Services Offer?
<--- Score

73. Is the quality assurance team identified?
<--- Score

74. What do you need to start doing?
<--- Score

75. How do you recognize an Services Offer objection?
<--- Score

76. What situation(s) led to this Services Offer Self Assessment?
<--- Score

77. Are your goals realistic? Do you need to redefine your problem? Perhaps the problem has changed or maybe you have reached your goal and need to set a new one?
<--- Score

78. What is the problem or issue?
<--- Score

79. What problems are you facing and how do you consider Services Offer will circumvent those obstacles?

<--- Score

80. Do you know what you need to know about Services Offer?
<--- Score

81. Is the need for organizational change recognized?
<--- Score

82. What tools and technologies are needed for a custom Services Offer project?
<--- Score

83. How are the Services Offer's objectives aligned to the group's overall stakeholder strategy?
<--- Score

84. How do you identify subcontractor relationships?
<--- Score

85. What are the Services Offer resources needed?
<--- Score

86. To what extent would your organization benefit from being recognized as a award recipient?
<--- Score

87. What is the smallest subset of the problem you can usefully solve?
<--- Score

88. How do you identify the kinds of information that you will need?
<--- Score

89. What is the recognized need?

<--- Score

90. Have you identified your Services Offer key performance indicators?
<--- Score

91. Do you need to avoid or amend any Services Offer activities?
<--- Score

92. What are the stakeholder objectives to be achieved with Services Offer?
<--- Score

93. As a sponsor, customer or management, how important is it to meet goals, objectives?
<--- Score

94. Which issues are too important to ignore?
<--- Score

95. What are the clients issues and concerns?
<--- Score

96. What is the problem and/or vulnerability?
<--- Score

97. Where is training needed?
<--- Score

98. How do you recognize an objection?
<--- Score

Add up total points for this section:
_ _ _ _ _ = Total points for this section

Divided by: _____ (number of
statements answered) = _____
Average score for this section

Transfer your score to the Services Offer
Index at the beginning of the Self-
Assessment.

CRITERION #2: DEFINE:

INTENT: Formulate the stakeholder problem. Define the problem, needs and objectives.

In my belief, the answer to this question is clearly defined:

5 Strongly Agree

4 Agree

3 Neutral

2 Disagree

1 Strongly Disagree

1. What are the boundaries of the scope? What is in bounds and what is not? What is the start point? What is the stop point?
<--- Score

2. Has everyone on the team, including the team leaders, been properly trained?
<--- Score

3. What specifically is the problem? Where does it occur? When does it occur? What is its extent?
<--- Score

4. Is the Services Offer scope manageable?
<--- Score

5. Why are you doing Services Offer and what is the scope?
<--- Score

6. How would you define the culture at your organization, how susceptible is it to Services Offer changes?
<--- Score

7. What baselines are required to be defined and managed?
<--- Score

8. What are the rough order estimates on cost savings/ opportunities that Services Offer brings?
<--- Score

9. Is there regularly 100% attendance at the team meetings? If not, have appointed substitutes attended to preserve cross-functionality and full representation?
<--- Score

10. Is the improvement team aware of the different versions of a process: what they think it is vs. what it actually is vs. what it should be vs. what it could be?
<--- Score

11. How are consistent Services Offer definitions

important?

<--- Score

12. What are the tasks and definitions?

<--- Score

13. Have the customer needs been translated into specific, measurable requirements? How?

<--- Score

14. What sort of initial information to gather?

<--- Score

15. What Services Offer requirements should be gathered?

<--- Score

16. What happens if Services Offer's scope changes?

<--- Score

17. Do you have a Services Offer success story or case study ready to tell and share?

<--- Score

18. Does the team have regular meetings?

<--- Score

19. How have you defined all Services Offer requirements first?

<--- Score

20. How was the 'as is' process map developed, reviewed, verified and validated?

<--- Score

21. How do you manage changes in Services Offer

requirements?
<--- Score

22. Is there a completed SIPOC representation, describing the Suppliers, Inputs, Process, Outputs, and Customers?
<--- Score

23. What is the scope of the Services Offer work?
<--- Score

24. What are the Roles and Responsibilities for each team member and its leadership? Where is this documented?
<--- Score

25. Has a team charter been developed and communicated?
<--- Score

26. What are the Services Offer use cases?
<--- Score

27. Is special Services Offer user knowledge required?
<--- Score

28. Is the work to date meeting requirements?
<--- Score

29. When is the estimated completion date?
<--- Score

30. How do you manage scope?
<--- Score

31. Is Services Offer linked to key stakeholder goals

and objectives?

<--- Score

32. How do you keep key subject matter experts in the loop?

<--- Score

33. Is there a clear Services Offer case definition?

<--- Score

34. How is the team tracking and documenting its work?

<--- Score

35. How does the Services Offer manager ensure against scope creep?

<--- Score

36. The political context: who holds power?

<--- Score

37. How do you think the partners involved in Services Offer would have defined success?

<--- Score

38. What are the requirements for audit information?

<--- Score

39. Are there different segments of customers?

<--- Score

40. What is out-of-scope initially?

<--- Score

41. Are the Services Offer requirements complete?

<--- Score

42. When is/was the Services Offer start date?

<--- Score

43. What key stakeholder process output measure(s) does Services Offer leverage and how?

<--- Score

44. Has the improvement team collected the 'voice of the customer' (obtained feedback – qualitative and quantitative)?

<--- Score

45. Are customer(s) identified and segmented according to their different needs and requirements?

<--- Score

46. Is Services Offer currently on schedule according to the plan?

<--- Score

47. Will a Services Offer production readiness review be required?

<--- Score

48. Are approval levels defined for contracts and supplements to contracts?

<--- Score

49. Who is gathering Services Offer information?

<--- Score

50. Does the scope remain the same?

<--- Score

51. Scope of sensitive information?

<--- Score

52. What are (control) requirements for Services Offer Information?
<--- Score

53. What sources do you use to gather information for a Services Offer study?
<--- Score

54. What critical content must be communicated – who, what, when, where, and how?
<--- Score

55. What scope to assess?
<--- Score

56. Is there a completed, verified, and validated high-level 'as is' (not 'should be' or 'could be') stakeholder process map?
<--- Score

57. Are roles and responsibilities formally defined?
<--- Score

58. What is the scope of Services Offer?
<--- Score

59. What is in the scope and what is not in scope?
<--- Score

60. Has a high-level 'as is' process map been completed, verified and validated?
<--- Score

61. Do you all define Services Offer in the same way?

<--- Score

62. How do you gather requirements?
<--- Score

63. Has a project plan, Gantt chart, or similar been developed/completed?
<--- Score

64. What are the core elements of the Services Offer business case?
<--- Score

65. How often are the team meetings?
<--- Score

66. When are meeting minutes sent out? Who is on the distribution list?
<--- Score

67. Are resources adequate for the scope?
<--- Score

68. What knowledge or experience is required?
<--- Score

69. What Services Offer services do you require?
<--- Score

70. How do you catch Services Offer definition inconsistencies?
<--- Score

71. What intelligence can you gather?
<--- Score

72. Has anyone else (internal or external to the group) attempted to solve this problem or a similar one before? If so, what knowledge can be leveraged from these previous efforts?
<--- Score

73. Have all basic functions of Services Offer been defined?
<--- Score

74. Is the scope of Services Offer defined?
<--- Score

75. Do the problem and goal statements meet the SMART criteria (specific, measurable, attainable, relevant, and time-bound)?
<--- Score

76. How do you hand over Services Offer context?
<--- Score

77. How can the value of Services Offer be defined?
<--- Score

78. Is there a critical path to deliver Services Offer results?
<--- Score

79. What information should you gather?
<--- Score

80. What would be the goal or target for a Services Offer's improvement team?
<--- Score

81. What is a worst-case scenario for losses?

<--- Score

82. How do you gather Services Offer requirements?
<--- Score

83. What is in scope?
<--- Score

84. What is the definition of Services Offer excellence?
<--- Score

85. Who approved the Services Offer scope?
<--- Score

86. What are the Services Offer tasks and definitions?
<--- Score

87. What are the record-keeping requirements of Services Offer activities?
<--- Score

88. Who defines (or who defined) the rules and roles?
<--- Score

89. Have all of the relationships been defined properly?
<--- Score

90. What constraints exist that might impact the team?
<--- Score

91. Who are the Services Offer improvement team members, including Management Leads and Coaches?
<--- Score

92. How will variation in the actual durations of each activity be dealt with to ensure that the expected Services Offer results are met?
<--- Score

93. How will the Services Offer team and the group measure complete success of Services Offer?
<--- Score

94. What is the context?
<--- Score

95. Is the current 'as is' process being followed? If not, what are the discrepancies?
<--- Score

96. What gets examined?
<--- Score

97. Has/have the customer(s) been identified?
<--- Score

98. Has the Services Offer work been fairly and/ or equitably divided and delegated among team members who are qualified and capable to perform the work? Has everyone contributed?
<--- Score

99. How and when will the baselines be defined?
<--- Score

100. How did the Services Offer manager receive input to the development of a Services Offer improvement plan and the estimated completion dates/times of each activity?

<--- Score

101. What are the compelling stakeholder reasons for embarking on Services Offer?
<--- Score

102. What is the definition of success?
<--- Score

103. What are the dynamics of the communication plan?
<--- Score

104. Is there any additional Services Offer definition of success?
<--- Score

105. Is the team equipped with available and reliable resources?
<--- Score

106. Is it clearly defined in and to your organization what you do?
<--- Score

107. How would you define Services Offer leadership?
<--- Score

108. Where can you gather more information?
<--- Score

109. Are task requirements clearly defined?
<--- Score

110. What was the context?
<--- Score

111. How do you build the right business case?
<--- Score

112. Has the direction changed at all during the course of Services Offer? If so, when did it change and why?
<--- Score

113. Are accountability and ownership for Services Offer clearly defined?
<--- Score

114. What customer feedback methods were used to solicit their input?
<--- Score

115. Has a Services Offer requirement not been met?
<--- Score

116. Are required metrics defined, what are they?
<--- Score

117. Are all requirements met?
<--- Score

118. What scope do you want your strategy to cover?
<--- Score

119. What system do you use for gathering Services Offer information?
<--- Score

120. Is there a Services Offer management charter, including stakeholder case, problem and goal statements, scope, milestones, roles and

responsibilities, communication plan?
<--- Score

121. Is Services Offer required?
<--- Score

122. If substitutes have been appointed, have they
been briefed on the Services Offer goals and received
regular communications as to the progress to date?
<--- Score

123. Has your scope been defined?
<--- Score

124. Are different versions of process maps needed to
account for the different types of inputs?
<--- Score

125. How do you manage unclear Services Offer
requirements?
<--- Score

126. What is the worst case scenario?
<--- Score

127. What is out of scope?
<--- Score

128. Is data collected and displayed to better
understand customer(s) critical needs and
requirements.
<--- Score

129. Is the team adequately staffed with the desired
cross-functionality? If not, what additional resources
are available to the team?

<--- Score

130. Are there any constraints known that bear on
the ability to perform Services Offer work? How is the
team addressing them?
<--- Score

Add up total points for this section:
_____ = Total points for this section

Divided by: _____ (number of
statements answered) = _____
Average score for this section

Transfer your score to the Services Offer
Index at the beginning of the Self-
Assessment.

CRITERION #3: MEASURE:

INTENT: Gather the correct data. Measure the current performance and evolution of the situation.

In my belief, the answer to this question is clearly defined:

5 Strongly Agree

4 Agree

3 Neutral

2 Disagree

1 Strongly Disagree

1. How is performance measured?
<--- Score

2. What is the cost of rework?
<--- Score

3. Are Services Offer vulnerabilities categorized and prioritized?
<--- Score

4. Do you have any cost Services Offer limitation requirements?
<--- Score

5. Are supply costs steady or fluctuating?
<--- Score

6. What is the Services Offer business impact?
<--- Score

7. What do you measure and why?
<--- Score

8. When should you bother with diagrams?
<--- Score

9. What causes mismanagement?
<--- Score

10. Where is the cost?
<--- Score

11. What could cause delays in the schedule?
<--- Score

12. Where is it measured?
<--- Score

13. What are the costs?
<--- Score

14. Have design-to-cost goals been established?
<--- Score

15. Are actual costs in line with budgeted costs?

<--- Score

16. How long to keep data and how to manage retention costs?
<--- Score

17. Is there an opportunity to verify requirements?
<--- Score

18. Are there measurements based on task performance?
<--- Score

19. How do you measure efficient delivery of Services Offer services?
<--- Score

20. What causes innovation to fail or succeed in your organization?
<--- Score

21. What does verifying compliance entail?
<--- Score

22. What is the cause of any Services Offer gaps?
<--- Score

23. Do the benefits outweigh the costs?
<--- Score

24. Why do you expend time and effort to implement measurement, for whom?
<--- Score

25. What measurements are possible, practicable and meaningful?

<--- Score

26. Is it possible to estimate the impact of unanticipated complexity such as wrong or failed assumptions, feedback, etcetera on proposed reforms?
<--- Score

27. How frequently do you track Services Offer measures?
<--- Score

28. Was a business case (cost/benefit) developed?
<--- Score

29. What are hidden Services Offer quality costs?
<--- Score

30. What do people want to verify?
<--- Score

31. What are you verifying?
<--- Score

32. What does your operating model cost?
<--- Score

33. What are the uncertainties surrounding estimates of impact?
<--- Score

34. What disadvantage does this cause for the user?
<--- Score

35. Does the Services Offer task fit the client's priorities?

<--- Score

36. Is the solution cost-effective?
<--- Score

37. Do you effectively measure and reward individual and team performance?
<--- Score

38. When a disaster occurs, who gets priority?
<--- Score

39. Are the units of measure consistent?
<--- Score

40. How will effects be measured?
<--- Score

41. What are the costs and benefits?
<--- Score

42. Do you have an issue in getting priority?
<--- Score

43. What causes investor action?
<--- Score

44. How do you control the overall costs of your work processes?
<--- Score

45. Are the measurements objective?
<--- Score

46. Are missed Services Offer opportunities costing your organization money?

<--- Score

47. How sensitive must the Services Offer strategy be to cost?
<--- Score

48. Who should receive measurement reports?
<--- Score

49. How do you verify the Services Offer requirements quality?
<--- Score

50. What are the Services Offer investment costs?
<--- Score

51. Who is involved in verifying compliance?
<--- Score

52. What are your customers expectations and measures?
<--- Score

53. How much does it cost?
<--- Score

54. How are measurements made?
<--- Score

55. What is the root cause(s) of the problem?
<--- Score

56. What would it cost to replace your technology?
<--- Score

57. What methods are feasible and acceptable to

estimate the impact of reforms?
<--- Score

58. What tests verify requirements?
<--- Score

59. What drives O&M cost?
<--- Score

60. Is the cost worth the Services Offer effort ?
<--- Score

61. What are the Services Offer key cost drivers?
<--- Score

62. How do you measure lifecycle phases?
<--- Score

63. What can be used to verify compliance?
<--- Score

64. What potential environmental factors impact the Services Offer effort?
<--- Score

65. Does a Services Offer quantification method exist?
<--- Score

66. How are costs allocated?
<--- Score

67. What are the estimated costs of proposed changes?
<--- Score

68. How do you verify and develop ideas and

innovations?
<--- Score

69. What is an unallowable cost?
<--- Score

70. Do you verify that corrective actions were taken?
<--- Score

71. How will you measure your Services Offer effectiveness?
<--- Score

72. What would be a real cause for concern?
<--- Score

73. What is your Services Offer quality cost segregation study?
<--- Score

74. What are your key Services Offer organizational performance measures, including key short and longer-term financial measures?
<--- Score

75. What are the types and number of measures to use?
<--- Score

76. What are the costs of reform?
<--- Score

77. How do you prevent mis-estimating cost?
<--- Score

78. How will your organization measure success?

<--- Score

79. How do you quantify and qualify impacts?
<--- Score

80. How do you verify and validate the Services Offer data?
<--- Score

81. How will success or failure be measured?
<--- Score

82. Have you made assumptions about the shape of the future, particularly its impact on your customers and competitors?
<--- Score

83. How will measures be used to manage and adapt?
<--- Score

84. What is the total fixed cost?
<--- Score

85. What evidence is there and what is measured?
<--- Score

86. When are costs are incurred?
<--- Score

87. Are there competing Services Offer priorities?
<--- Score

88. How do you measure variability?
<--- Score

89. What are your operating costs?

<--- Score

90. Are the Services Offer benefits worth its costs?
<--- Score

91. How do you verify performance?
<--- Score

92. What details are required of the Services Offer cost structure?
<--- Score

93. What measurements are being captured?
<--- Score

94. What are allowable costs?
<--- Score

95. What does losing customers cost your organization?
<--- Score

96. Does management have the right priorities among projects?
<--- Score

97. What users will be impacted?
<--- Score

98. Do you aggressively reward and promote the people who have the biggest impact on creating excellent Services Offer services/products?
<--- Score

99. How do you aggregate measures across priorities?
<--- Score

100. How is the value delivered by Services Offer being measured?
<--- Score

101. Do you have a flow diagram of what happens?
<--- Score

102. Where can you go to verify the info?
<--- Score

103. What are your primary costs, revenues, assets?
<--- Score

104. How can you measure the performance?
<--- Score

105. Are there any easy-to-implement alternatives to Services Offer? Sometimes other solutions are available that do not require the cost implications of a full-blown project?
<--- Score

106. Which measures and indicators matter?
<--- Score

107. How can a Services Offer test verify your ideas or assumptions?
<--- Score

108. How will you measure success?
<--- Score

109. What are the current costs of the Services Offer process?
<--- Score

110. How can you measure Services Offer in a systematic way?
<--- Score

111. Have you included everything in your Services Offer cost models?
<--- Score

112. How can you reduce costs?
<--- Score

113. Are you able to realize any cost savings?
<--- Score

114. Are you taking your company in the direction of better and revenue or cheaper and cost?
<--- Score

115. What are the strategic priorities for this year?
<--- Score

116. How do you verify Services Offer completeness and accuracy?
<--- Score

117. How frequently do you verify your Services Offer strategy?
<--- Score

118. Are you aware of what could cause a problem?
<--- Score

119. How can you reduce the costs of obtaining inputs?
<--- Score

120. Which costs should be taken into account?
<--- Score

121. How will costs be allocated?
<--- Score

122. Why do the measurements/indicators matter?
<--- Score

123. What could cause you to change course?
<--- Score

124. What is your decision requirements diagram?
<--- Score

125. How do you verify your resources?
<--- Score

126. Are indirect costs charged to the Services Offer program?
<--- Score

127. What is the total cost related to deploying Services Offer, including any consulting or professional services?
<--- Score

128. What does a Test Case verify?
<--- Score

129. Who pays the cost?
<--- Score

130. Did you tackle the cause or the symptom?
<--- Score

Add up total points for this section:
_____ = Total points for this section

Divided by: _____ (number of
statements answered) = _____
Average score for this section

Transfer your score to the Services Offer
Index at the beginning of the Self-
Assessment.

CRITERION #4: ANALYZE:

INTENT: Analyze causes, assumptions and hypotheses.

In my belief, the answer to this question is clearly defined:

5 Strongly Agree

4 Agree

3 Neutral

2 Disagree

1 Strongly Disagree

1. What are your best practices for minimizing Services Offer project risk, while demonstrating incremental value and quick wins throughout the Services Offer project lifecycle?
<--- Score

2. What is the Services Offer Driver?
<--- Score

3. Have the problem and goal statements been

updated to reflect the additional knowledge gained from the analyze phase?
<--- Score

4. What output to create?
<--- Score

5. Has data output been validated?
<--- Score

6. What are the revised rough estimates of the financial savings/opportunity for Services Offer improvements?
<--- Score

7. What internal processes need improvement?
<--- Score

8. How do your work systems and key work processes relate to and capitalize on your core competencies?
<--- Score

9. What are the personnel training and qualifications required?
<--- Score

10. How do you identify specific Services Offer investment opportunities and emerging trends?
<--- Score

11. How do you promote understanding that opportunity for improvement is not criticism of the status quo, or the people who created the status quo?
<--- Score

12. Did any additional data need to be collected?

<--- Score

13. What process should you select for improvement?
<--- Score

14. Should you invest in industry-recognized qualifications?
<--- Score

15. Were Pareto charts (or similar) used to portray the 'heavy hitters' (or key sources of variation)?
<--- Score

16. Have any additional benefits been identified that will result from closing all or most of the gaps?
<--- Score

17. Is there any way to speed up the process?
<--- Score

18. Where is Services Offer data gathered?
<--- Score

19. Is the suppliers process defined and controlled?
<--- Score

20. Are all staff in core Services Offer subjects Highly Qualified?
<--- Score

21. What systems/processes must you excel at?
<--- Score

22. Were there any improvement opportunities identified from the process analysis?
<--- Score

23. Do your contracts/agreements contain data security obligations?
<--- Score

24. A compounding model resolution with available relevant data can often provide insight towards a solution methodology; which Services Offer models, tools and techniques are necessary?
<--- Score

25. What are the best opportunities for value improvement?
<--- Score

26. How difficult is it to qualify what Services Offer ROI is?
<--- Score

27. What is your organizations system for selecting qualified vendors?
<--- Score

28. Do you have the authority to produce the output?
<--- Score

29. Do your leaders quickly bounce back from setbacks?
<--- Score

30. Who gets your output?
<--- Score

31. Who is involved in the management review process?
<--- Score

32. Is there an established change management process?
<--- Score

33. What are the Services Offer design outputs?
<--- Score

34. What are the disruptive Services Offer technologies that enable your organization to radically change your business processes?
<--- Score

35. Think about some of the processes you undertake within your organization, which do you own?
<--- Score

36. Did any value-added analysis or 'lean thinking' take place to identify some of the gaps shown on the 'as is' process map?
<--- Score

37. How are outputs preserved and protected?
<--- Score

38. What Services Offer data should be collected?
<--- Score

39. What is the output?
<--- Score

40. What other jobs or tasks affect the performance of the steps in the Services Offer process?
<--- Score

41. How will the Services Offer data be captured?

<--- Score

42. What conclusions were drawn from the team's data collection and analysis? How did the team reach these conclusions?
<--- Score

43. How has the Services Offer data been gathered?
<--- Score

44. Do staff qualifications match your project?
<--- Score

45. Is data and process analysis, root cause analysis and quantifying the gap/opportunity in place?
<--- Score

46. What will drive Services Offer change?
<--- Score

47. Have you defined which data is gathered how?
<--- Score

48. What are your current levels and trends in key measures or indicators of Services Offer product and process performance that are important to and directly serve your customers? How do these results compare with the performance of your competitors and other organizations with similar offerings?
<--- Score

49. What data is gathered?
<--- Score

50. What is your organizations process which leads to recognition of value generation?

<--- Score

51. What are your outputs?
<--- Score

52. What tools were used to narrow the list of possible causes?
<--- Score

53. Can you add value to the current Services Offer decision-making process (largely qualitative) by incorporating uncertainty modeling (more quantitative)?
<--- Score

54. How many input/output points does it require?
<--- Score

55. What are evaluation criteria for the output?
<--- Score

56. What quality tools were used to get through the analyze phase?
<--- Score

57. What Services Offer data should be managed?
<--- Score

58. Was a cause-and-effect diagram used to explore the different types of causes (or sources of variation)?
<--- Score

59. How was the detailed process map generated, verified, and validated?
<--- Score

60. How is Services Offer data gathered?
<--- Score

61. Who owns what data?
<--- Score

62. What resources go in to get the desired output?
<--- Score

63. How will the data be checked for quality?
<--- Score

64. What did the team gain from developing a sub-process map?
<--- Score

65. Is the required Services Offer data gathered?
<--- Score

66. What is the complexity of the output produced?
<--- Score

67. Identify an operational issue in your organization, for example, could a particular task be done more quickly or more efficiently by Services Offer?
<--- Score

68. What is the oversight process?
<--- Score

69. How can risk management be tied procedurally to process elements?
<--- Score

70. How do you implement and manage your work processes to ensure that they meet design

requirements?

<--- Score

71. Do you understand your management processes today?

<--- Score

72. How do you measure the operational performance of your key work systems and processes, including productivity, cycle time, and other appropriate measures of process effectiveness, efficiency, and innovation?

<--- Score

73. What data do you need to collect?

<--- Score

74. What qualifies as competition?

<--- Score

75. Is the performance gap determined?

<--- Score

76. When should a process be art not science?

<--- Score

77. Are Services Offer changes recognized early enough to be approved through the regular process?

<--- Score

78. Are gaps between current performance and the goal performance identified?

<--- Score

79. What qualifications are necessary?

<--- Score

80. What is the Value Stream Mapping?
<--- Score

81. What information qualified as important?
<--- Score

82. Is the final output clearly identified?
<--- Score

83. What qualifications do Services Offer leaders need?
<--- Score

84. Think about the functions involved in your Services Offer project, what processes flow from these functions?
<--- Score

85. What are the necessary qualifications?
<--- Score

86. What successful thing are you doing today that may be blinding you to new growth opportunities?
<--- Score

87. What methods do you use to gather Services Offer data?
<--- Score

88. What were the crucial 'moments of truth' on the process map?
<--- Score

89. Who will facilitate the team and process?
<--- Score

90. What, related to, Services Offer processes does your organization outsource?
<--- Score

91. Which Services Offer data should be retained?
<--- Score

92. Is the Services Offer process severely broken such that a re-design is necessary?
<--- Score

93. What qualifications are needed?
<--- Score

94. What kind of crime could a potential new hire have committed that would not only not disqualify him/her from being hired by your organization, but would actually indicate that he/she might be a particularly good fit?
<--- Score

95. An organizationally feasible system request is one that considers the mission, goals and objectives of the organization, key questions are: is the Services Offer solution request practical and will it solve a problem or take advantage of an opportunity to achieve company goals?
<--- Score

96. How much data can be collected in the given timeframe?
<--- Score

97. What Services Offer metrics are outputs of the process?

<--- Score

98. What types of data do your Services Offer indicators require?
<--- Score

99. Are all team members qualified for all tasks?
<--- Score

100. Where is the data coming from to measure compliance?
<--- Score

101. How do you ensure that the Services Offer opportunity is realistic?
<--- Score

102. Do you, as a leader, bounce back quickly from setbacks?
<--- Score

103. What are your current levels and trends in key Services Offer measures or indicators of product and process performance that are important to and directly serve your customers?
<--- Score

104. What Services Offer data will be collected?
<--- Score

105. How is the way you as the leader think and process information affecting your organizational culture?
<--- Score

106. What do you need to qualify?

<--- Score

107. How will corresponding data be collected?
<--- Score

108. Do your employees have the opportunity to do what they do best everyday?
<--- Score

109. Are you missing Services Offer opportunities?
<--- Score

110. What training and qualifications will you need?
<--- Score

111. Were any designed experiments used to generate additional insight into the data analysis?
<--- Score

112. What is the cost of poor quality as supported by the team's analysis?
<--- Score

113. What process improvements will be needed?
<--- Score

114. Who is involved with workflow mapping?
<--- Score

115. What were the financial benefits resulting from any 'ground fruit or low-hanging fruit' (quick fixes)?
<--- Score

116. What are your Services Offer processes?
<--- Score

117. What controls do you have in place to protect data?
<--- Score

118. Is the gap/opportunity displayed and communicated in financial terms?
<--- Score

119. How often will data be collected for measures?
<--- Score

120. What does the data say about the performance of the stakeholder process?
<--- Score

121. Who will gather what data?
<--- Score

122. How do you define collaboration and team output?
<--- Score

123. Record-keeping requirements flow from the records needed as inputs, outputs, controls and for transformation of a Services Offer process, are the records needed as inputs to the Services Offer process available?
<--- Score

124. Who qualifies to gain access to data?
<--- Score

125. Is pre-qualification of suppliers carried out?
<--- Score

126. What tools were used to generate the list of

possible causes?
<--- Score

127. What are the processes for audit reporting and management?
<--- Score

128. Do several people in different organizational units assist with the Services Offer process?
<--- Score

129. How do you use Services Offer data and information to support organizational decision making and innovation?
<--- Score

130. Is there a strict change management process?
<--- Score

131. How do mission and objectives affect the Services Offer processes of your organization?
<--- Score

132. How is the Services Offer Value Stream Mapping managed?
<--- Score

133. What qualifications and skills do you need?
<--- Score

134. How will the change process be managed?
<--- Score

135. Was a detailed process map created to amplify critical steps of the 'as is' stakeholder process?
<--- Score

136. How is data used for program management and improvement?
<--- Score

Add up total points for this section:
_____ = Total points for this section

Divided by: _____ (number of statements answered) = _____
Average score for this section

Transfer your score to the Services Offer Index at the beginning of the Self-Assessment.

CRITERION #5: IMPROVE:

INTENT: Develop a practical solution. Innovate, establish and test the solution and to measure the results.

In my belief, the answer to this question is clearly defined:

5 Strongly Agree

4 Agree

3 Neutral

2 Disagree

1 Strongly Disagree

1. What tools do you use once you have decided on a Services Offer strategy and more importantly how do you choose?
<--- Score

2. How will you measure the results?
<--- Score

3. How significant is the improvement in the eyes of

the end user?
<--- Score

4. Can you identify any significant risks or exposures to Services Offer third- parties (vendors, service providers, alliance partners etc) that concern you?
<--- Score

5. To what extent does management recognize Services Offer as a tool to increase the results?
<--- Score

6. What is the Services Offer's sustainability risk?
<--- Score

7. How do you improve productivity?
<--- Score

8. What went well, what should change, what can improve?
<--- Score

9. Services Offer risk decisions: whose call Is It?
<--- Score

10. How can the phases of Services Offer development be identified?
<--- Score

11. Do you combine technical expertise with business knowledge and Services Offer Key topics include lifecycles, development approaches, requirements and how to make a business case?
<--- Score

12. What criteria will you use to assess your Services

Offer risks?
<--- Score

13. Where do you need Services Offer improvement?
<--- Score

14. Explorations of the frontiers of Services Offer will help you build influence, improve Services Offer, optimize decision making, and sustain change, what is your approach?
<--- Score

15. Who are the key stakeholders for the Services Offer evaluation?
<--- Score

16. Where do the Services Offer decisions reside?
<--- Score

17. What is the magnitude of the improvements?
<--- Score

18. How risky is your organization?
<--- Score

19. Would you develop a Services Offer Communication Strategy?
<--- Score

20. What current systems have to be understood and/ or changed?
<--- Score

21. Who are the Services Offer decision makers?
<--- Score

22. Are the risks fully understood, reasonable and manageable?
<--- Score

23. What are the implications of the one critical Services Offer decision 10 minutes, 10 months, and 10 years from now?
<--- Score

24. How are policy decisions made and where?
<--- Score

25. How do you define the solutions' scope?
<--- Score

26. Do vendor agreements bring new compliance risk ?
<--- Score

27. Who will be using the results of the measurement activities?
<--- Score

28. Who will be responsible for making the decisions to include or exclude requested changes once Services Offer is underway?
<--- Score

29. What lessons, if any, from a pilot were incorporated into the design of the full-scale solution?
<--- Score

30. How are Services Offer risks managed?
<--- Score

31. What risks do you need to manage?

<--- Score

32. How do you mitigate Services Offer risk?
<--- Score

33. How do the Services Offer results compare with the performance of your competitors and other organizations with similar offerings?
<--- Score

34. Who manages supplier risk management in your organization?
<--- Score

35. What were the criteria for evaluating a Services Offer pilot?
<--- Score

36. How do you go about comparing Services Offer approaches/solutions?
<--- Score

37. How do you manage and improve your Services Offer work systems to deliver customer value and achieve organizational success and sustainability?
<--- Score

38. How do you manage Services Offer risk?
<--- Score

39. Are decisions made in a timely manner?
<--- Score

40. How do you decide how much to remunerate an employee?
<--- Score

41. Does a good decision guarantee a good outcome?
<--- Score

42. Was a Services Offer charter developed?
<--- Score

43. Are risk triggers captured?
<--- Score

44. Are events managed to resolution?
<--- Score

45. Is any Services Offer documentation required?
<--- Score

46. Are the key business and technology risks being managed?
<--- Score

47. When you map the key players in your own work and the types/domains of relationships with them, which relationships do you find easy and which challenging, and why?
<--- Score

48. Who makes the Services Offer decisions in your organization?
<--- Score

49. Are procedures documented for managing Services Offer risks?
<--- Score

50. For decision problems, how do you develop a decision statement?

<--- Score

51. Do employees understand the products and services offered by your organization?
<--- Score

52. Do you have the optimal project management team structure?
<--- Score

53. How is continuous improvement applied to risk management?
<--- Score

54. How will you recognize and celebrate results?
<--- Score

55. What are the concrete Services Offer results?
<--- Score

56. Who are the Services Offer decision-makers?
<--- Score

57. How do you keep improving Services Offer?
<--- Score

58. What can you do to improve?
<--- Score

59. How can you better manage risk?
<--- Score

60. What tools were used to tap into the creativity and encourage 'outside the box' thinking?
<--- Score

61. Is the Services Offer risk managed?
<--- Score

62. What are your current levels and trends in key measures or indicators of workforce and leader development?
<--- Score

63. What are the Services Offer security risks?
<--- Score

64. Can you integrate quality management and risk management?
<--- Score

65. What is Services Offer risk?
<--- Score

66. Are you assessing Services Offer and risk?
<--- Score

67. How do you deal with Services Offer risk?
<--- Score

68. Is risk periodically assessed?
<--- Score

69. Have you identified breakpoints and/or risk tolerances that will trigger broad consideration of a potential need for intervention or modification of strategy?
<--- Score

70. How can you improve Services Offer?
<--- Score

71. What alternative responses are available to manage risk?
<--- Score

72. How does the team improve its work?
<--- Score

73. Who controls the risk?
<--- Score

74. What are the expected Services Offer results?
<--- Score

75. Have you achieved Services Offer improvements?
<--- Score

76. Who are the people involved in developing and implementing Services Offer?
<--- Score

77. What needs improvement? Why?
<--- Score

78. Which Services Offer solution is appropriate?
<--- Score

79. Who controls key decisions that will be made?
<--- Score

80. Risk Identification: What are the possible risk events your organization faces in relation to Services Offer?
<--- Score

81. Can the solution be designed and implemented within an acceptable time period?

<--- Score

82. Is there any other Services Offer solution?
<--- Score

83. What tools were used to evaluate the potential solutions?
<--- Score

84. What assumptions are made about the solution and approach?
<--- Score

85. Is Services Offer documentation maintained?
<--- Score

86. If you could go back in time five years, what decision would you make differently? What is your best guess as to what decision you're making today you might regret five years from now?
<--- Score

87. Is the Services Offer solution sustainable?
<--- Score

88. Do those selected for the Services Offer team have a good general understanding of what Services Offer is all about?
<--- Score

89. What tools were most useful during the improve phase?
<--- Score

90. What are the affordable Services Offer risks?
<--- Score

91. Is the Services Offer documentation thorough?
<--- Score

92. How do you improve Services Offer service perception, and satisfaction?
<--- Score

93. How do you link measurement and risk?
<--- Score

94. Do you need to do a usability evaluation?
<--- Score

95. What improvements have been achieved?
<--- Score

96. Are risk management tasks balanced centrally and locally?
<--- Score

97. What should a proof of concept or pilot accomplish?
<--- Score

98. Risk events: what are the things that could go wrong?
<--- Score

99. How do you improve your likelihood of success ?
<--- Score

100. How can skill-level changes improve Services Offer?
<--- Score

101. How will you know that a change is an improvement?
<--- Score

102. Are the most efficient solutions problem-specific?
<--- Score

103. How will you know that you have improved?
<--- Score

104. How do you measure risk?
<--- Score

105. How will you know when its improved?
<--- Score

106. Is supporting Services Offer documentation required?
<--- Score

107. Who do you report Services Offer results to?
<--- Score

108. Who manages Services Offer risk?
<--- Score

109. What practices helps your organization to develop its capacity to recognize patterns?
<--- Score

110. What area needs the greatest improvement?
<--- Score

111. For estimation problems, how do you develop an estimation statement?
<--- Score

112. What strategies for Services Offer improvement are successful?
<--- Score

113. Risk factors: what are the characteristics of Services Offer that make it risky?
<--- Score

114. Will the controls trigger any other risks?
<--- Score

115. What is the risk?
<--- Score

116. How do you measure progress and evaluate training effectiveness?
<--- Score

117. Is the solution technically practical?
<--- Score

118. What resources are required for the improvement efforts?
<--- Score

119. How do you measure improved Services Offer service perception, and satisfaction?
<--- Score

120. Do you cover the five essential competencies: Communication, Collaboration,Innovation, Adaptability, and Leadership that improve an organizations ability to leverage the new Services Offer in a volatile global economy?
<--- Score

121. Is there a high likelihood that any recommendations will achieve their intended results?
<--- Score

122. What were the underlying assumptions on the cost-benefit analysis?
<--- Score

123. How does your organization evaluate strategic Services Offer success?
<--- Score

124. How can you improve performance?
<--- Score

125. What to do with the results or outcomes of measurements?
<--- Score

126. Who will be responsible for documenting the Services Offer requirements in detail?
<--- Score

127. In the past few months, what is the smallest change you have made that has had the biggest positive result? What was it about that small change that produced the large return?
<--- Score

128. What actually has to improve and by how much?
<--- Score

129. How scalable is your Services Offer solution?
<--- Score

130. What Services Offer improvements can be made?
<--- Score

131. How is knowledge sharing about risk management improved?
<--- Score

132. Which of the recognised risks out of all risks can be most likely transferred?
<--- Score

Add up total points for this section:
_ _ _ _ _ = Total points for this section

Divided by: _ _ _ _ _ _ (number of statements answered) = _ _ _ _ _ _
Average score for this section

Transfer your score to the Services Offer Index at the beginning of the Self-Assessment.

CRITERION #6: CONTROL:

INTENT: Implement the practical solution. Maintain the performance and correct possible complications.

In my belief, the answer to this question is clearly defined:

5 Strongly Agree

4 Agree

3 Neutral

2 Disagree

1 Strongly Disagree

1. Act/Adjust: What Do you Need to Do Differently?
<--- Score

2. What should the next improvement project be that is related to Services Offer?
<--- Score

3. What is the best design framework for Services Offer organization now that, in a post industrial-age

if the top-down, command and control model is no longer relevant?

<--- Score

4. How will report readings be checked to effectively monitor performance?

<--- Score

5. Is there a Services Offer Communication plan covering who needs to get what information when?

<--- Score

6. Is there a standardized process?

<--- Score

7. How widespread is its use?

<--- Score

8. How will the process owner and team be able to hold the gains?

<--- Score

9. Are operating procedures consistent?

<--- Score

10. How will the day-to-day responsibilities for monitoring and continual improvement be transferred from the improvement team to the process owner?

<--- Score

11. What are the key elements of your Services Offer performance improvement system, including your evaluation, organizational learning, and innovation processes?

<--- Score

12. How is change control managed?
<--- Score

13. What is the recommended frequency of auditing?
<--- Score

14. What are you attempting to measure/monitor?
<--- Score

15. Against what alternative is success being measured?
<--- Score

16. Who has control over resources?
<--- Score

17. What is the standard for acceptable Services Offer performance?
<--- Score

18. Are pertinent alerts monitored, analyzed and distributed to appropriate personnel?
<--- Score

19. Is there a transfer of ownership and knowledge to process owner and process team tasked with the responsibilities.
<--- Score

20. How do controls support value?
<--- Score

21. How will Services Offer decisions be made and monitored?
<--- Score

22. Is there a documented and implemented monitoring plan?
<--- Score

23. How do you establish and deploy modified action plans if circumstances require a shift in plans and rapid execution of new plans?
<--- Score

24. What quality tools were useful in the control phase?
<--- Score

25. Can support from partners be adjusted?
<--- Score

26. Will the team be available to assist members in planning investigations?
<--- Score

27. Implementation Planning: is a pilot needed to test the changes before a full roll out occurs?
<--- Score

28. What Services Offer standards are applicable?
<--- Score

29. Are new process steps, standards, and documentation ingrained into normal operations?
<--- Score

30. What is the control/monitoring plan?
<--- Score

31. Are there documented procedures?

<--- Score

32. How do you monitor usage and cost?
<--- Score

33. Are the planned controls working?
<--- Score

34. Do you monitor the Services Offer decisions made and fine tune them as they evolve?
<--- Score

35. Do the Services Offer decisions you make today help people and the planet tomorrow?
<--- Score

36. Is knowledge gained on process shared and institutionalized?
<--- Score

37. Do the viable solutions scale to future needs?
<--- Score

38. Does job training on the documented procedures need to be part of the process team's education and training?
<--- Score

39. How will the process owner verify improvement in present and future sigma levels, process capabilities?
<--- Score

40. What are the known security controls?
<--- Score

41. What do your reports reflect?

<--- Score

42. How do you plan for the cost of succession?
<--- Score

43. What should you measure to verify efficiency gains?
<--- Score

44. Has the improved process and its steps been standardized?
<--- Score

45. Who sets the Services Offer standards?
<--- Score

46. How do senior leaders actions reflect a commitment to the organizations Services Offer values?
<--- Score

47. Will existing staff require re-training, for example, to learn new business processes?
<--- Score

48. Does a troubleshooting guide exist or is it needed?
<--- Score

49. How likely is the current Services Offer plan to come in on schedule or on budget?
<--- Score

50. Who controls critical resources?
<--- Score

51. What key inputs and outputs are being measured

on an ongoing basis?
<--- Score

52. Will any special training be provided for results interpretation?
<--- Score

53. What is your plan to assess your security risks?
<--- Score

54. In the case of a Services Offer project, the criteria for the audit derive from implementation objectives, an audit of a Services Offer project involves assessing whether the recommendations outlined for implementation have been met, can you track that any Services Offer project is implemented as planned, and is it working?
<--- Score

55. Is there a control plan in place for sustaining improvements (short and long-term)?
<--- Score

56. Are documented procedures clear and easy to follow for the operators?
<--- Score

57. Does Services Offer appropriately measure and monitor risk?
<--- Score

58. What are the critical parameters to watch?
<--- Score

59. How do you plan on providing proper recognition and disclosure of supporting companies?

<--- Score

60. What other areas of the group might benefit from the Services Offer team's improvements, knowledge, and learning?
<--- Score

61. Does the Services Offer performance meet the customer's requirements?
<--- Score

62. How do you encourage people to take control and responsibility?
<--- Score

63. What do you measure to verify effectiveness gains?
<--- Score

64. Is the Services Offer test/monitoring cost justified?
<--- Score

65. Is reporting being used or needed?
<--- Score

66. Can you adapt and adjust to changing Services Offer situations?
<--- Score

67. What can you control?
<--- Score

68. Is there a recommended audit plan for routine surveillance inspections of Services Offer's gains?
<--- Score

69. How can you best use all of your knowledge repositories to enhance learning and sharing?
<--- Score

70. Is there an action plan in case of emergencies?
<--- Score

71. What are customers monitoring?
<--- Score

72. How is Services Offer project cost planned, managed, monitored?
<--- Score

73. Does the response plan contain a definite closed loop continual improvement scheme (e.g., plan-do-check-act)?
<--- Score

74. Who is the Services Offer process owner?
<--- Score

75. How do your controls stack up?
<--- Score

76. Will your goals reflect your program budget?
<--- Score

77. What are your results for key measures or indicators of the accomplishment of your Services Offer strategy and action plans, including building and strengthening core competencies?
<--- Score

78. What other systems, operations, processes, and infrastructures (hiring practices, staffing, training,

incentives/rewards, metrics/dashboards/scorecards, etc.) need updates, additions, changes, or deletions in order to facilitate knowledge transfer and improvements?
<--- Score

79. Do you monitor the effectiveness of your Services Offer activities?
<--- Score

80. What are the performance and scale of the Services Offer tools?
<--- Score

81. Is there documentation that will support the successful operation of the improvement?
<--- Score

82. Is a response plan established and deployed?
<--- Score

83. Is new knowledge gained imbedded in the response plan?
<--- Score

84. Are suggested corrective/restorative actions indicated on the response plan for known causes to problems that might surface?
<--- Score

85. How might the group capture best practices and lessons learned so as to leverage improvements?
<--- Score

86. You may have created your quality measures at a time when you lacked resources, technology wasn't

up to the required standard, or low service levels were the industry norm. Have those circumstances changed?

<--- Score

87. How do you spread information?

<--- Score

88. How will you measure your QA plan's effectiveness?

<--- Score

89. Is a response plan in place for when the input, process, or output measures indicate an 'out-of-control' condition?

<--- Score

90. How do you select, collect, align, and integrate Services Offer data and information for tracking daily operations and overall organizational performance, including progress relative to strategic objectives and action plans?

<--- Score

91. Are the planned controls in place?

<--- Score

92. Have new or revised work instructions resulted?

<--- Score

93. Are controls in place and consistently applied?

<--- Score

94. Do the provider services offer fine grained access control?

<--- Score

95. Has the Services Offer value of standards been quantified?
<--- Score

96. Where do ideas that reach policy makers and planners as proposals for Services Offer strengthening and reform actually originate?
<--- Score

97. What adjustments to the strategies are needed?
<--- Score

98. How will new or emerging customer needs/requirements be checked/communicated to orient the process toward meeting the new specifications and continually reducing variation?
<--- Score

99. How will input, process, and output variables be checked to detect for sub-optimal conditions?
<--- Score

100. What is your theory of human motivation, and how does your compensation plan fit with that view?
<--- Score

Add up total points for this section:
_ _ _ _ _ = Total points for this section

Divided by: _ _ _ _ _ _ (number of statements answered) = _ _ _ _ _ _
Average score for this section

Transfer your score to the Services Offer Index at the beginning of the Self-

Assessment.

CRITERION #7: SUSTAIN:

INTENT: Retain the benefits.

In my belief, the answer to this
question is clearly defined:

5 Strongly Agree

4 Agree

3 Neutral

2 Disagree

1 Strongly Disagree

1. Instead of going to current contacts for new ideas,
what if you reconnected with dormant contacts--
the people you used to know? If you were going
reactivate a dormant tie, who would it be?
<--- Score

2. What does your signature ensure?
<--- Score

3. What must you excel at?
<--- Score

4. Did your employees make progress today?
<--- Score

5. Is there any reason to believe the opposite of my current belief?
<--- Score

6. Ask yourself: how would you do this work if you only had one staff member to do it?
<--- Score

7. What is effective Services Offer?
<--- Score

8. Who else should you help?
<--- Score

9. How do you make it meaningful in connecting Services Offer with what users do day-to-day?
<--- Score

10. Which models, tools and techniques are necessary?
<--- Score

11. What is the overall business strategy?
<--- Score

12. Do you think you know, or do you know you know ?
<--- Score

13. How will you know that the Services Offer project has been successful?
<--- Score

14. Is there any existing Services Offer governance structure?
<--- Score

15. What are the long-term Services Offer goals?
<--- Score

16. Who are your customers?
<--- Score

17. Whom among your colleagues do you trust, and for what?
<--- Score

18. Who are four people whose careers you have enhanced?
<--- Score

19. How is implementation research currently incorporated into each of your goals?
<--- Score

20. Product/service: how competitive and successful are the goods and services offered by the vendor in this market?
<--- Score

21. Why is Services Offer important for you now?
<--- Score

22. Do you have an implicit bias for capital investments over people investments?
<--- Score

23. What would have to be true for the option on the

table to be the best possible choice?
<--- Score

24. What is the funding source for this project?
<--- Score

25. Have you used any facility related services offered by a private organization/firm?
<--- Score

26. What information is critical to your organization that your executives are ignoring?
<--- Score

27. What are the essentials of internal Services Offer management?
<--- Score

28. What may be the consequences for the performance of an organization if all stakeholders are not consulted regarding Services Offer?
<--- Score

29. What are the key enablers to make this Services Offer move?
<--- Score

30. Who are the key stakeholders?
<--- Score

31. How do you maintain Services Offer's Integrity?
<--- Score

32. At what moment would you think; Will I get fired?
<--- Score

33. What counts that you are not counting?
<--- Score

34. What is something you believe that nearly no one agrees with you on?
<--- Score

35. Can you do all this work?
<--- Score

36. How do you track customer value, profitability or financial return, organizational success, and sustainability?
<--- Score

37. How do you keep the momentum going?
<--- Score

38. How do you transition from the baseline to the target?
<--- Score

39. Where can you break convention?
<--- Score

40. What is the source of the strategies for Services Offer strengthening and reform?
<--- Score

41. What are the barriers to increased Services Offer production?
<--- Score

42. Are you making progress, and are you making progress as Services Offer leaders?
<--- Score

43. What is your BATNA (best alternative to a negotiated agreement)?
<--- Score

44. Is your basic point _____ or _____?
<--- Score

45. Is the Services Offer organization completing tasks effectively and efficiently?
<--- Score

46. What is the estimated value of the project?
<--- Score

47. What are the challenges?
<--- Score

48. Are the assumptions believable and achievable?
<--- Score

49. What Services Offer skills are most important?
<--- Score

50. Who is on the team?
<--- Score

51. How can you negotiate Services Offer successfully with a stubborn boss, an irate client, or a deceitful coworker?
<--- Score

52. Are you / should you be revolutionary or evolutionary?
<--- Score

53. What is the kind of project structure that would be appropriate for your Services Offer project, should it be formal and complex, or can it be less formal and relatively simple?
<--- Score

54. Who will use the services offered by the service systems?
<--- Score

55. Whose voice (department, ethnic group, women, older workers, etc) might you have missed hearing from in your company, and how might you amplify this voice to create positive momentum for your business?
<--- Score

56. What will be the consequences to the stakeholder (financial, reputation etc) if Services Offer does not go ahead or fails to deliver the objectives?
<--- Score

57. Which individuals, teams or departments will be involved in Services Offer?
<--- Score

58. In a project to restructure Services Offer outcomes, which stakeholders would you involve?
<--- Score

59. What Services Offer modifications can you make work for you?
<--- Score

60. What are your most important goals for the strategic Services Offer objectives?

<--- Score

61. What are the top 3 things at the forefront of your Services Offer agendas for the next 3 years?
<--- Score

62. What is a feasible sequencing of reform initiatives over time?
<--- Score

63. Operational - will it work?
<--- Score

64. Do you know what you are doing? And who do you call if you don't?
<--- Score

65. Why not do Services Offer?
<--- Score

66. What are the success criteria that will indicate that Services Offer objectives have been met and the benefits delivered?
<--- Score

67. How will you insure seamless interoperability of Services Offer moving forward?
<--- Score

68. How can you incorporate support to ensure safe and effective use of Services Offer into the services that you provide?
<--- Score

69. Do you say no to customers for no reason?
<--- Score

70. What relationships among Services Offer trends do you perceive?
<--- Score

71. What role does communication play in the success or failure of a Services Offer project?
<--- Score

72. If there were zero limitations, what would you do differently?
<--- Score

73. Will there be any necessary staff changes (redundancies or new hires)?
<--- Score

74. What are specific Services Offer rules to follow?
<--- Score

75. What goals did you miss?
<--- Score

76. What is the range of capabilities?
<--- Score

77. What is the customers perception of the quality and types of services offered?
<--- Score

78. If you do not follow, then how to lead?
<--- Score

79. What business benefits will Services Offer goals deliver if achieved?
<--- Score

80. How do you ensure that implementations of Services Offer products are done in a way that ensures safety?
<--- Score

81. How do you lead with Services Offer in mind?
<--- Score

82. Are assumptions made in Services Offer stated explicitly?
<--- Score

83. When information truly is ubiquitous, when reach and connectivity are completely global, when computing resources are infinite, and when a whole new set of impossibilities are not only possible, but happening, what will that do to your business?
<--- Score

84. What happens if you do not have enough funding?
<--- Score

85. How important is Services Offer to the user organizations mission?
<--- Score

86. Do you have enough freaky customers in your portfolio pushing you to the limit day in and day out?
<--- Score

87. How do you proactively clarify deliverables and Services Offer quality expectations?
<--- Score

88. What are you challenging?
<--- Score

89. What is the craziest thing you can do?
<--- Score

90. Is Services Offer dependent on the successful delivery of a current project?
<--- Score

91. If you had to rebuild your organization without any traditional competitive advantages (i.e., no killer technology, promising research, innovative product/ service delivery model, etcetera), how would your people have to approach their work and collaborate together in order to create the necessary conditions for success?
<--- Score

92. What is your formula for success in Services Offer ?
<--- Score

93. In the past year, what have you done (or could you have done) to increase the accurate perception of your company/brand as ethical and honest?
<--- Score

94. How do customers see your organization?
<--- Score

95. What was the last experiment you ran?
<--- Score

96. How long will it take to change?
<--- Score

97. What are the potential basics of Services Offer fraud?
<--- Score

98. Do you have past Services Offer successes?
<--- Score

99. Think of your Services Offer project, what are the main functions?
<--- Score

100. Why is it important to have senior management support for a Services Offer project?
<--- Score

101. How do you provide a safe environment -physically and emotionally?
<--- Score

102. Who is responsible for ensuring appropriate resources (time, people and money) are allocated to Services Offer?
<--- Score

103. How do you govern and fulfill your societal responsibilities?
<--- Score

104. What is your question? Why?
<--- Score

105. Who is the main stakeholder, with ultimate responsibility for driving Services Offer forward?
<--- Score

106. How will you ensure you get what you expected?

<--- Score

107. Who will be responsible for deciding whether Services Offer goes ahead or not after the initial investigations?
<--- Score

108. Who do we want your customers to become?
<--- Score

109. What are your personal philosophies regarding Services Offer and how do they influence your work?
<--- Score

110. How do you create buy-in?
<--- Score

111. Who have you, as a company, historically been when you've been at your best?
<--- Score

112. Are all key stakeholders present at all Structured Walkthroughs?
<--- Score

113. Who is responsible for Services Offer?
<--- Score

114. How do you engage the workforce, in addition to satisfying them?
<--- Score

115. How much contingency will be available in the budget?
<--- Score

116. Will it be accepted by users?
<--- Score

117. If your customer were your grandmother, would you tell her to buy what you're selling?
<--- Score

118. How do you foster innovation?
<--- Score

119. What projects are going on in the organization today, and what resources are those projects using from the resource pools?
<--- Score

120. Do you think Services Offer accomplishes the goals you expect it to accomplish?
<--- Score

121. What potential megatrends could make your business model obsolete?
<--- Score

122. What trophy do you want on your mantle?
<--- Score

123. How do you keep records, of what?
<--- Score

124. Which Services Offer goals are the most important?
<--- Score

125. What unique value proposition (UVP) do you offer?
<--- Score

126. What are the short and long-term Services Offer goals?

<--- Score

127. Why do and why don't your customers like your organization?

<--- Score

128. What do sas remote managed software and services offer?

<--- Score

129. How will you motivate the stakeholders with the least vested interest?

<--- Score

130. How do you deal with Services Offer changes?

<--- Score

131. If you weren't already in this business, would you enter it today? And if not, what are you going to do about it?

<--- Score

132. Is maximizing Services Offer protection the same as minimizing Services Offer loss?

<--- Score

133. Do you feel that more should be done in the Services Offer area?

<--- Score

134. How do you stay inspired?

<--- Score

135. What should you stop doing?
<--- Score

136. How do you set Services Offer stretch targets and how do you get people to not only participate in setting these stretch targets but also that they strive to achieve these?
<--- Score

137. What trouble can you get into?
<--- Score

138. Do you have the right people on the bus?
<--- Score

139. Is a Services Offer team work effort in place?
<--- Score

140. What are the major products and services offered by the call centre/helpdesk staff to the customers?
<--- Score

141. How can you become the company that would put you out of business?
<--- Score

142. Is there a work around that you can use?
<--- Score

143. What are internal and external Services Offer relations?
<--- Score

144. What is the recommended frequency of auditing?
<--- Score

145. How do senior leaders deploy your organizations vision and values through your leadership system, to the workforce, to key suppliers and partners, and to customers and other stakeholders, as appropriate?
<--- Score

146. In retrospect, of the projects that you pulled the plug on, what percent do you wish had been allowed to keep going, and what percent do you wish had ended earlier?
<--- Score

147. You have the right catalog of services offered to a given customer?
<--- Score

148. If no one would ever find out about your accomplishments, how would you lead differently?
<--- Score

149. How do you determine the key elements that affect Services Offer workforce satisfaction, how are these elements determined for different workforce groups and segments?
<--- Score

150. Are you maintaining a past–present–future perspective throughout the Services Offer discussion?
<--- Score

151. What are the products and services offered?
<--- Score

152. Why should people listen to you?
<--- Score

153. What are the gaps in your knowledge and experience?
<--- Score

154. Who uses your product in ways you never expected?
<--- Score

155. Who will provide the final approval of Services Offer deliverables?
<--- Score

156. If you find that you havent accomplished one of the goals for one of the steps of the Services Offer strategy, what will you do to fix it?
<--- Score

157. Political -is anyone trying to undermine this project?
<--- Score

158. Can you maintain your growth without detracting from the factors that have contributed to your success?
<--- Score

159. How do you accomplish your long range Services Offer goals?
<--- Score

160. Who, on the executive team or the board, has spoken to a customer recently?
<--- Score

161. What are current Services Offer paradigms?

<--- Score

162. Which functions and people interact with the supplier and or customer?
<--- Score

163. What is the purpose of Services Offer in relation to the mission?
<--- Score

164. What happens at your organization when people fail?
<--- Score

165. Who do you think the world wants your organization to be?
<--- Score

166. How can you become more high-tech but still be high touch?
<--- Score

167. Is it economical; do you have the time and money?
<--- Score

168. What happens when a new employee joins the organization?
<--- Score

169. What management system can you use to leverage the Services Offer experience, ideas, and concerns of the people closest to the work to be done?
<--- Score

170. Is Services Offer realistic, or are you setting yourself up for failure?
<--- Score

171. Would you rather sell to knowledgeable and informed customers or to uninformed customers?
<--- Score

172. If you got fired and a new hire took your place, what would she do different?
<--- Score

173. How are you doing compared to your industry?
<--- Score

174. How do you go about securing Services Offer?
<--- Score

175. To whom do you add value?
<--- Score

176. How do you foster the skills, knowledge, talents, attributes, and characteristics you want to have?
<--- Score

177. Marketing budgets are tighter, consumers are more skeptical, and social media has changed forever the way we talk about Services Offer, how do you gain traction?
<--- Score

178. What are you trying to prove to yourself, and how might it be hijacking your life and business success?
<--- Score

179. What stupid rule would you most like to kill?

<--- Score

180. Do you have the right capabilities and capacities?
<--- Score

181. What range of services offered?
<--- Score

182. How do you know if you are successful?
<--- Score

183. What are the business goals Services Offer is aiming to achieve?
<--- Score

184. If you were responsible for initiating and implementing major changes in your organization, what steps might you take to ensure acceptance of those changes?
<--- Score

185. What are strategies for increasing support and reducing opposition?
<--- Score

186. Are the criteria for selecting recommendations stated?
<--- Score

187. What is it like to work for you?
<--- Score

188. Is your strategy driving your strategy? Or is the way in which you allocate resources driving your strategy?
<--- Score

189. What are the warranty provisions for the goods/services offered?
<--- Score

190. What is your competitive advantage?
<--- Score

191. If you had to leave your organization for a year and the only communication you could have with employees/colleagues was a single paragraph, what would you write?
<--- Score

192. What you are going to do to affect the numbers?
<--- Score

193. Who is responsible for errors?
<--- Score

194. Who do you want your customers to become?
<--- Score

195. What is your Services Offer strategy?
<--- Score

Add up total points for this section:
_____ = Total points for this section

Divided by: _____ (number of statements answered) = _____
Average score for this section

Transfer your score to the Services Offer Index at the beginning of the Self-Assessment.

Services Offer and Managing Projects, Criteria for Project Managers:

1.0 Initiating Process Group: Services Offer

1. Establishment of pm office?

2. What communication items need improvement?

3. The Services Offer project you are managing has nine stakeholders. How many channel of communications are there between corresponding stakeholders?

4. Are you just doing busywork to pass the time?

5. What is the stake of others in your Services Offer project?

6. What will you do to minimize the impact should a risk event occur?

7. How is each deliverable reviewed, verified, and validated?

8. How well did the chosen processes produce the expected results?

9. Who is involved in each phase?

10. Are you properly tracking the progress of the Services Offer project and communicating the status to stakeholders?

11. What were things that you need to improve?

12. Do you know if the Services Offer project requires

outside equipment or vendor resources?

13. Are you certain deliverables are properly completed and meet quality standards?

14. Who is performing the work of the Services Offer project?

15. How can you make your needs known?

16. What will you do?

17. What are the constraints?

18. Who are the Services Offer project stakeholders?

19. What will be the pressing issues of tomorrow?

1.1 Project Charter: Services Offer

20. Customer benefits: what customer requirements does this Services Offer project address?

21. Why is it important?

22. Assumptions and constraints: what assumptions were made in defining the Services Offer project?

23. What is the most common tool for helping define the detail?

24. How will you know that a change is an improvement?

25. Who is the sponsor?

26. Is it an improvement over existing products?

27. What changes can you make to improve?

28. How high should you set your goals?

29. Services Offer project objective statement: what must the Services Offer project do?

30. For whom?

31. Who manages integration?

32. What goes into your Services Offer project Charter?

33. Why Outsource?

34. Does the Services Offer project need to consider any special capacity or capability issues?

35. When will this occur?

36. Why do you need to manage scope?

37. Who is the Services Offer project Manager?

38. Are you building in-house ?

39. Who are the stakeholders?

1.2 Stakeholder Register: Services Offer

40. What is the power of the stakeholder?

41. What opportunities exist to provide communications?

42. Is your organization ready for change?

43. What & Why?

44. What are the major Services Offer project milestones requiring communications or providing communications opportunities?

45. Who is managing stakeholder engagement?

46. How big is the gap?

47. How much influence do they have on the Services Offer project?

48. How will reports be created?

49. Who wants to talk about Security?

50. How should employers make voices heard?

1.3 Stakeholder Analysis Matrix: Services Offer

51. Disadvantages of proposition?

52. New markets, vertical, horizontal?

53. Advantages of proposition?

54. What is your Advocacy Strategy?

55. How much do resources cost?

56. Innovative aspects?

57. Management cover, succession?

58. What do you need to appraise?

59. What is the stakeholders name, what is function?

60. Economy - home, abroad?

61. How do customers express needs?

62. Morale, commitment, leadership?

63. Who is most interested in information about the topic and/or has previously initiated interest?

64. Location and geographical?

65. Why do you care?

66. What unique or lowest-cost resources does the Services Offer project have access to?

67. Continuity, supply chain robustness?

68. How affected by the problem(s)?

69. Arena: in what fields are the actors active, where are they present?

2.0 Planning Process Group: Services Offer

70. When will the Services Offer project be done?

71. What should you do next?

72. What makes your Services Offer project successful?

73. What is a Software Development Life Cycle (SDLC)?

74. To what extent do the intervention objectives and strategies of the Services Offer project respond to your organizations plans?

75. Does the program have follow-up mechanisms (to verify the quality of the products, punctuality of delivery, etc.) to measure progress in the achievement of the envisaged results?

76. How are it Services Offer projects different?

77. Is the identification of the problems, inequalities and gaps, with respective causes, clear in the Services Offer project?

78. What do you need to do?

79. How will users learn how to use the deliverables?

80. To what extent are the participating departments coordinating with each other?

81. In which Services Offer project management process group is the detailed Services Offer project budget created?

82. On which process should team members spend the most time?

83. How many days can task X be late in starting without affecting the Services Offer project completion date?

84. What is involved in Services Offer project scope management, and why is good Services Offer project scope management so important on information technology Services Offer projects?

85. What factors are contributing to progress or delay in the achievement of products and results?

86. To what extent have the target population and participants made the activities own, taking an active role in it?

87. Did the program design/ implementation strategy adequately address the planning stage necessary to set up structures, hire staff etc.?

88. In what way has the Services Offer project come up with innovative measures for problem-solving?

89. How well do the team follow the chosen processes?

2.1 Project Management Plan: Services Offer

90. What data/reports/tools/etc. do your PMs need?

91. What are the assumptions?

92. Was the peer (technical) review of the cost estimates duly coordinated with the cost estimate center of expertise and addressed in the review documentation and certification?

93. What goes into your Services Offer project Charter?

94. Are there any Client staffing expectations?

95. Who is the Services Offer project Manager?

96. Did the planning effort collaborate to develop solutions that integrate expertise, policies, programs, and Services Offer projects across entities?

97. How do you manage integration?

98. When is a Services Offer project management plan created?

99. Do there need to be organizational changes?

100. Is the budget realistic?

101. Is mitigation authorized or recommended?

102. How do you manage time?

103. What are the assigned resources?

104. Will you add a schedule and diagram?

105. How well are you able to manage your risk?

2.2 Scope Management Plan: Services Offer

106. Have Services Offer project success criteria been defined?

107. Is the steering committee active in Services Offer project oversight?

108. What is the need the Services Offer project will address?

109. Describe how the deliverables will be verified against the Services Offer project scope. To whom will the deliverables be first presented for inspection and verification?

110. How are you planning to maintain the scope baseline and how will you manage scope changes?

111. What is the relative power of the Services Offer project manager?

112. Are software metrics formally captured, analyzed and used as a basis for other Services Offer project estimates?

113. Are you doing what you have set out to do?

114. Have the procedures for identifying variances from estimates & adjusting the detailed work program been followed?

115. Has process improvement efforts been completed before requirements efforts begin?

116. Timeline and milestones?

117. Given the scope of the Services Offer project, which criterion should be optimized?

118. During what part of the PM process is the Services Offer project scope statement created?

119. Are changes in deliverable commitments agreed to by all affected groups & individuals?

120. Are corrective actions and variances reported?

121. What happens if scope changes?

122. Have the scope, objectives, costs, benefits and impacts been communicated to all involved and/or impacted stakeholders and work groups?

123. Have key stakeholders been identified?

124. Is current scope of the Services Offer project substantially different than that originally defined?

125. Has a resource management plan been created?

2.3 Requirements Management Plan: Services Offer

126. Is infrastructure setup part of your Services Offer project?

127. Will the Services Offer project requirements become approved in writing?

128. Why manage requirements?

129. Who will finally present the work or product(s) for acceptance?

130. Could inaccurate or incomplete requirements in this Services Offer project create a serious risk for the business?

131. Controlling Services Offer project requirements involves monitoring the status of the Services Offer project requirements and managing changes to the requirements. Who is responsible for monitoring and tracking the Services Offer project requirements?

132. When and how will a requirements baseline be established in this Services Offer project?

133. Will you document changes to requirements?

134. Who has the authority to reject Services Offer project requirements?

135. After the requirements are gathered and set

forth on the requirements register, theyre little more than a laundry list of items. Some may be duplicates, some might conflict with others and some will be too broad or too vague to understand. Describe how the requirements will be analyzed. Who will perform the analysis?

136. If it exists, where is it housed?

137. Did you get proper approvals?

138. Will you perform a Requirements Risk assessment and develop a plan to deal with risks?

139. How will unresolved questions be handled once approval has been obtained?

140. How knowledgeable is the primary Stakeholder(s) in the proposed application area?

141. Subject to change control?

142. Should you include sub-activities?

143. Define the help desk model. who will take full responsibility?

144. Is any organizational data being used or stored?

145. Is stakeholder risk tolerance an important factor for the requirements process in this Services Offer project?

2.4 Requirements Documentation: Services Offer

146. Are all functions required by the customer included?

147. What happens when requirements are wrong?

148. What if the system wasn t implemented?

149. How does what is being described meet the business need?

150. What kind of entity is a problem ?

151. Where do system and software requirements come from, what are sources?

152. Do your constraints stand?

153. Consistency. are there any requirements conflicts?

154. Do technical resources exist?

155. Who is interacting with the system?

156. What is the risk associated with cost and schedule?

157. Validity. does the system provide the functions which best support the customers needs?

158. What are the attributes of a customer?

159. How do you know when a Requirement is accurate enough?

160. Does the system provide the functions which best support the customers needs?

161. How to document system requirements?

162. Verifiability. can the requirements be checked?

163. Are there legal issues?

164. What are the potential disadvantages/ advantages?

165. How much does requirements engineering cost?

2.5 Requirements Traceability Matrix: Services Offer

166. Why use a WBS?

167. Describe the process for approving requirements so they can be added to the traceability matrix and Services Offer project work can be performed. Will the Services Offer project requirements become approved in writing?

168. Do you have a clear understanding of all subcontracts in place?

169. What are the chronologies, contingencies, consequences, criteria?

170. How will it affect the stakeholders personally in career?

171. What percentage of Services Offer projects are producing traceability matrices between requirements and other work products?

172. Will you use a Requirements Traceability Matrix?

173. What is the WBS?

174. Is there a requirements traceability process in place?

175. How do you manage scope?

176. How small is small enough?

177. Why do you manage scope?

2.6 Project Scope Statement: Services Offer

178. Services Offer project lead, team lead, solution architect?

179. How often will scope changes be reviewed?

180. What process would you recommend for creating the Services Offer project scope statement?

181. What are the defined meeting materials?

182. Has the format for tracking and monitoring schedules and costs been defined?

183. Has a method and process for requirement tracking been developed?

184. What are the major deliverables of the Services Offer project?

185. What is the product of this Services Offer project?

186. Will the risk plan be updated on a regular and frequent basis?

187. Is there an information system for the Services Offer project?

188. Who will you recommend approve the change, and when do you recommend the change reviews occur?

189. Will this process be communicated to the customer and Services Offer project team?

190. Will all tasks resulting from issues be entered into the Services Offer project Plan and tracked through the plan?

191. How will you verify the accuracy of the work of the Services Offer project, and what constitutes acceptance of the deliverables?

192. Is the plan under configuration management?

193. If there are vendors, have they signed off on the Services Offer project Plan?

194. Elements of scope management that deal with concept development ?

195. Is the plan for Services Offer project resources adequate?

196. Is the plan for your organization of the Services Offer project resources adequate?

2.7 Assumption and Constraint Log: Services Offer

197. Can you perform this task or activity in a more effective manner?

198. Are there processes in place to ensure that all the terms and code concepts have been documented consistently?

199. Are formal code reviews conducted?

200. Has the approach and development strategy of the Services Offer project been defined, documented and accepted by the appropriate stakeholders?

201. Does a documented Services Offer project organizational policy & plan (i.e. governance model) exist?

202. What weaknesses do you have?

203. What is positive about the current process?

204. Does the document/deliverable meet all requirements (for example, statement of work) specific to this deliverable?

205. Have all stakeholders been identified?

206. If appropriate, is the deliverable content consistent with current Services Offer project documents and in compliance with the Document

Management Plan?

207. Is staff trained on the software technologies that are being used on the Services Offer project?

208. Is there adequate stakeholder participation for the vetting of requirements definition, changes and management?

209. Are there processes in place to ensure internal consistency between the source code components?

210. Is the process working, and people are not executing in compliance of the process?

211. What do you log?

212. Contradictory information between different documents?

213. What strengths do you have?

214. Are there unnecessary steps that are creating bottlenecks and/or causing people to wait?

215. Are there nonconformance issues?

216. Can the requirements be traced to the appropriate components of the solution, as well as test scripts?

2.8 Work Breakdown Structure: Services Offer

217. Where does it take place?

218. How much detail?

219. Is the work breakdown structure (wbs) defined and is the scope of the Services Offer project clear with assigned deliverable owners?

220. What is the probability of completing the Services Offer project in less that xx days?

221. When does it have to be done?

222. Who has to do it?

223. Can you make it?

224. When do you stop?

225. When would you develop a Work Breakdown Structure?

226. Do you need another level?

227. Is it still viable?

228. Is it a change in scope?

229. How big is a work-package?

230. What is the probability that the Services Offer project duration will exceed xx weeks?

231. How will you and your Services Offer project team define the Services Offer projects scope and work breakdown structure?

232. What has to be done?

2.9 WBS Dictionary: Services Offer

233. Appropriate work authorization documents which subdivide the contractual effort and responsibilities, within functional organizations?

234. Does the contractors system provide for the determination of cost variances attributable to the excess usage of material?

235. Are all affected work authorizations, budgeting, and scheduling documents amended to properly reflect the effects of authorized changes?

236. Identify potential or actual overruns and underruns?

237. Are budgets or values assigned to work packages and planning packages in terms of dollars, hours, or other measurable units?

238. Are the procedures for identifying indirect costs to incurring organizations, indirect cost pools, and allocating the costs from the pools to the contracts formally documented?

239. Identify potential or actual budget-based and time-based schedule variances?

240. Are the contractors estimates of costs at completion reconcilable with cost data reported to us?

241. Are the bases and rates for allocating costs from

each indirect pool to commercial work consistent with the already stated used to allocate corresponding costs to Government contracts?

242. Are the overhead pools formally and adequately identified?

243. Are your organizations and items of cost assigned to each pool identified?

244. All cwbs elements specified for external reporting?

245. Does the contractors system provide unit costs, equivalent unit or lot costs in terms of labor, material, other direct, and indirect costs?

246. Are all elements of indirect expense identified to overhead cost budgets of Services Offer projections?

247. Are the latest revised estimates of costs at completion compared with the established budgets at appropriate levels and causes of variances identified?

248. Are authorized changes being incorporated in a timely manner?

249. Are retroactive changes to direct costs and indirect costs prohibited except for the correction of errors and routine accounting adjustments?

250. Is work progressively subdivided into detailed work packages as requirements are defined?

2.10 Schedule Management Plan: Services Offer

251. Are meeting objectives identified for each meeting?

252. Are tasks tracked by hours?

253. Does the ims include all contract and/or designated management control milestones?

254. Are Services Offer project leaders committed to this Services Offer project full time?

255. What will be the final cost of the Services Offer project if status quo is maintained?

256. Does the ims reflect accurate current status and credible start/finish forecasts for all to-go tasks and milestones?

257. Does the resource management plan include a personnel development plan?

258. Is the schedule vertically and horizontally traceable?

259. Is Services Offer project status reviewed with the steering and executive teams at appropriate intervals?

260. Is there a set of procedures defining the scope, procedures, and deliverables defining quality control?

261. Cost / benefit analysis?

262. Time for overtime?

263. Can be realistically shortened (the duration of subsequent tasks)?

264. Do Services Offer project managers participating in the Services Offer project know the Services Offer projects true status first hand?

265. Are updated Services Offer project time & resource estimates reasonable based on the current Services Offer project stage?

266. Are scheduled deliverables actually delivered?

267. Which status reports are received per the Services Offer project Plan?

268. Why conduct schedule analysis?

269. Pareto diagrams, statistical sampling, flow charting or trend analysis used quality monitoring?

270. Are internal Services Offer project status meetings held at reasonable intervals?

2.11 Activity List: Services Offer

271. Are the required resources available or need to be acquired?

272. When do the individual activities need to start and finish?

273. Who will perform the work?

274. What went wrong?

275. How can the Services Offer project be displayed graphically to better visualize the activities?

276. The wbs is developed as part of a joint planning session. and how do you know that youhave done this right?

277. What went well?

278. What is the probability the Services Offer project can be completed in xx weeks?

279. How detailed should a Services Offer project get?

280. How will it be performed?

281. What is the LF and LS for each activity?

282. What are the critical bottleneck activities?

283. How should ongoing costs be monitored to try to keep the Services Offer project within budget?

284. Is there anything planned that does not need to be here?

285. What is the total time required to complete the Services Offer project if no delays occur?

286. How difficult will it be to do specific activities on this Services Offer project?

287. How do you determine the late start (LS) for each activity?

288. What are you counting on?

289. What will be performed?

2.12 Activity Attributes: Services Offer

290. What went right?

291. Do you feel very comfortable with your prediction?

292. Is there a trend during the year?

293. Have you identified the Activity Leveling Priority code value on each activity?

294. Why?

295. What activity do you think you should spend the most time on?

296. How many days do you need to complete the work scope with a limit of X number of resources?

297. What conclusions/generalizations can you draw from this?

298. How else could the items be grouped?

299. How difficult will it be to complete specific activities on this Services Offer project?

300. Are the required resources available?

301. Which method produces the more accurate cost assignment?

302. What is the general pattern here?

303. Resource is assigned to?

304. Were there other ways you could have organized the data to achieve similar results?

305. How many resources do you need to complete the work scope within a limit of X number of days?

306. How difficult will it be to do specific activities on this Services Offer project?

307. What is missing?

308. Resources to accomplish the work?

2.13 Milestone List: Services Offer

309. Sustainable financial backing?

310. Can you derive how soon can the whole Services Offer project finish?

311. Political effects?

312. Timescales, deadlines and pressures?

313. Information and research?

314. Vital contracts and partners?

315. Sustaining internal capabilities?

316. Calculate how long can activity be delayed?

317. How will you get the word out to customers?

318. Own known vulnerabilities?

319. Gaps in capabilities?

320. How soon can the activity start?

321. Identify critical paths (one or more) and which activities are on the critical path?

322. Legislative effects?

323. How will the milestone be verified?

324. How soon can the activity finish?

325. How late can each activity be finished and started?

326. It is to be a narrative text providing the crucial aspects of your Services Offer project proposal answering what, who, how, when and where?

2.14 Network Diagram: Services Offer

327. If x is long, what would be the completion time if you break x into two parallel parts of y weeks and z weeks?

328. If the Services Offer project network diagram cannot change and you have extra personnel resources, what is the BEST thing to do?

329. What job or jobs follow it?

330. What is the completion time?

331. What are the tools?

332. Can you calculate the confidence level?

333. What job or jobs precede it?

334. What must be completed before an activity can be started?

335. Will crashing x weeks return more in benefits than it costs?

336. Where do you schedule uncertainty time?

337. What activity must be completed immediately before this activity can start?

338. What job or jobs could run concurrently?

339. Are the gantt chart and/or network diagram

updated periodically and used to assess the overall Services Offer project timetable?

340. What activities must occur simultaneously with this activity?

341. Why must you schedule milestones, such as reviews, throughout the Services Offer project?

342. If a current contract exists, can you provide the vendor name, contract start, and contract expiration date?

343. What can be done concurrently?

344. What controls the start and finish of a job?

345. Planning: who, how long, what to do?

346. How difficult will it be to do specific activities on this Services Offer project?

2.15 Activity Resource Requirements: Services Offer

347. Which logical relationship does the PDM use most often?

348. Organizational Applicability?

349. Are there unresolved issues that need to be addressed?

350. What is the Work Plan Standard?

351. How do you handle petty cash?

352. Do you use tools like decomposition and rolling-wave planning to produce the activity list and other outputs?

353. When does monitoring begin?

354. Anything else?

355. What are constraints that you might find during the Human Resource Planning process?

356. Other support in specific areas?

357. How many signatures do you require on a check and does this match what is in your policy and procedures?

358. Why do you do that?

2.16 Resource Breakdown Structure: Services Offer

359. Why is this important?

360. What defines a successful Services Offer project?

361. Which resources should be in the resource pool?

362. Changes based on input from stakeholders?

363. Who is allowed to perform which functions?

364. Which resource planning tool provides information on resource responsibility and accountability?

365. What is the primary purpose of the human resource plan?

366. Who is allowed to see what data about which resources?

367. Is predictive resource analysis being done?

368. How difficult will it be to do specific activities on this Services Offer project?

369. What can you do to improve productivity?

370. What is your organizations history in doing similar activities?

371. Why time management?

372. When do they need the information?

373. How can this help you with team building?

374. Any changes from stakeholders?

375. Why do you do it?

2.17 Activity Duration Estimates: Services Offer

376. Are activity duration estimates documented?

377. What are two suggestions for ensuring adequate change control on Services Offer projects that involve outside contracts?

378. Write a oneto two-page paper describing your dream team for this Services Offer project. What type of people would you want on your team?

379. Is a contract change control system defined to manage changes to contract terms and conditions?

380. Does a process exist to determine the potential loss or gain if risk events occur?

381. Can they use the already stated?

382. How do functionality, system outputs, performance, reliability, and maintainability requirements affect quality planning?

383. What questions do you have about the sample documents provided?

384. Which does one need in order to complete schedule development?

385. How difficult will it be to do specific activities on this Services Offer project?

386. Are updates on work results collected and used as inputs to the performance reporting process?

387. Are tools and techniques defined for gathering, integrating and distributing Services Offer project outputs?

388. Have most organizations benefited from outsourcing?

389. What are the ways to create and distribute Services Offer project performance information?

390. Which is a benefit of an analogous Services Offer project estimate?

391. Calculate the expected duration for an activity that has a most likely time of 3, a pessimistic time of 10, and a optimiztic time of 2?

392. Do they make sense?

393. Is the work performed reviewed against contractual objectives?

394. How is the Services Offer project doing?

395. What do corresponding sources say about Services Offer project management?

2.18 Duration Estimating Worksheet: Services Offer

396. Why estimate costs?

397. Small or large Services Offer project?

398. Will the Services Offer project collaborate with the local community and leverage resources?

399. Is the Services Offer project responsive to community need?

400. For other activities, how much delay can be tolerated?

401. What info is needed?

402. Is a construction detail attached (to aid in explanation)?

403. What is the total time required to complete the Services Offer project if no delays occur?

404. What questions do you have?

405. What is your role?

406. What work will be included in the Services Offer project?

407. What utility impacts are there?

408. When does your organization expect to be able to complete it?

409. What is next?

410. What is an Average Services Offer project?

411. Done before proceeding with this activity or what can be done concurrently?

2.19 Project Schedule: Services Offer

412. How can you address that situation?

413. Why is this particularly bad?

414. Is the structure for tracking the Services Offer project schedule well defined and assigned to a specific individual?

415. What is risk management?

416. To what degree is do you feel the entire team was committed to the Services Offer project schedule?

417. Did the final product meet or exceed user expectations?

418. What is risk?

419. Activity charts and bar charts are graphical representations of a Services Offer project schedule ...how do they differ?

420. Change management required?

421. Is the Services Offer project schedule available for all Services Offer project team members to review?

422. Have all Services Offer project delays been adequately accounted for, communicated to all stakeholders and adjustments made in overall Services Offer project schedule?

423. Understand the constraints used in preparing the schedule. Are activities connected because logic dictates the order in which others occur?

424. Is infrastructure setup part of your Services Offer project?

425. What is the difference?

426. How can you minimize or control changes to Services Offer project schedules?

427. Are activities connected because logic dictates the order in which others occur?

428. If you can not fix it, how do you do it differently?

429. Your best shot for providing estimations how complex/how much work does the activity require?

430. Is Services Offer project work proceeding in accordance with the original Services Offer project schedule?

2.20 Cost Management Plan: Services Offer

431. Are the Services Offer project team members located locally to the users/stakeholders?

432. Are vendor contract reports, reviews and visits conducted periodically?

433. Does the detailed work plan match the complexity of tasks with the capabilities of personnel?

434. Have the reasons why the changes to your organizational systems and capabilities are required?

435. Environmental management – what changes in statutory environmental compliance requirements are anticipated during the Services Offer project?

436. Weve met your goals?

437. Is your organization certified as a broker of the products/supplies?

438. Cost estimate preparation – What cost estimates will be prepared during the Services Offer project phases?

439. Alignment to strategic goals & objectives?

440. Is it a Services Offer project?

441. Are enough systems & user personnel assigned

to the Services Offer project?

442. Are adequate resources provided for the quality assurance function?

443. Have the key functions and capabilities been defined and assigned to each release or iteration?

444. Have the procedures for identifying budget variances been followed?

445. What is Services Offer project cost management?

446. Is Services Offer project work proceeding in accordance with the original Services Offer project schedule?

447. Are the people assigned to the Services Offer project sufficiently qualified?

448. Has a sponsor been identified?

449. Published materials?

2.21 Activity Cost Estimates: Services Offer

450. Will you need to provide essential services information about activities?

451. Does the activity rely on a common set of tools to carry it out?

452. Does the estimator estimate by task or by person?

453. How many activities should you have?

454. How do you treat administrative costs in the activity inventory?

455. Can you change your activities?

456. Estimated cost?

457. Does the activity serve a common type of customer?

458. What skill level is required to do the job?

459. What is the activity inventory?

460. How difficult will it be to do specific tasks on the Services Offer project?

461. How do you fund change orders?

462. Where can you get activity reports?

463. Specific - is the objective clear in terms of what, how, when, and where the situation will be changed?

464. What happens if you cannot produce the documentation for the single audit?

465. Certification of actual expenditures?

466. What defines a successful Services Offer project?

467. What makes a good expected result statement?

468. Maintenance Reserve?

469. Are data needed on characteristics of care?

2.22 Cost Estimating Worksheet: Services Offer

470. Who is best positioned to know and assist in identifying corresponding factors?

471. Is it feasible to establish a control group arrangement?

472. What is the estimated labor cost today based upon this information?

473. Ask: are others positioned to know, are others credible, and will others cooperate?

474. Value pocket identification & quantification what are value pockets?

475. How will the results be shared and to whom?

476. What happens to any remaining funds not used?

477. What is the purpose of estimating?

478. Identify the timeframe necessary to monitor progress and collect data to determine how the selected measure has changed?

479. What costs are to be estimated?

480. What additional Services Offer project(s) could be initiated as a result of this Services Offer project?

481. Will the Services Offer project collaborate with the local community and leverage resources?

482. What can be included?

483. Can a trend be established from historical performance data on the selected measure and are the criteria for using trend analysis or forecasting methods met?

484. Is the Services Offer project responsive to community need?

485. Does the Services Offer project provide innovative ways for stakeholders to overcome obstacles or deliver better outcomes?

486. What will others want?

2.23 Cost Baseline: Services Offer

487. Have the actual milestone completion dates been compared to the approved schedule?

488. Is request in line with priorities?

489. Has the Services Offer project documentation been archived or otherwise disposed as described in the Services Offer project communication plan?

490. Are there contingencies or conditions related to the acceptance?

491. At which frequency ?

492. Is there anything you need from upper management in order to be successful?

493. Review your risk triggers -have your risks changed?

494. What is it ?

495. Is there anything unique in this Services Offer projects scope statement that will affect resources?

496. On time?

497. What is your organizations history in doing similar tasks?

498. Have all approved changes to the schedule baseline been identified and impact on the Services

Offer project documented?

499. Eac -estimate at completion, what is the total job expected to cost?

500. How likely is it to go wrong?

501. Does a process exist for establishing a cost baseline to measure Services Offer project performance?

502. How difficult will it be to do specific tasks on the Services Offer project?

503. How do you manage cost?

504. Has training and knowledge transfer of the operations organization been completed?

505. Has the appropriate access to relevant data and analysis capability been granted?

2.24 Quality Management Plan: Services Offer

506. You know what your customers expectations are regarding this process?

507. How are senior leaders, employees, and your organization involved in supporting the community?

508. Is this process still needed?

509. How do you manage quality?

510. Do you keep back-up copies of any data?

511. Who gets results of work?

512. What is the return on investment?

513. Does a documented Services Offer project organizational policy & plan (i.e. governance model) exist?

514. Are you meeting your customers expectations consistently?

515. Does the plan conform to standards?

516. What procedures are used to determine if you use, and the number of split, replicate or duplicate samples taken at a site?

517. Can it be done better?

518. How do your action plans support the strategic objectives?

519. Does the program conduct field testing?

520. How are deviations from procedures handled?

521. How do you measure?

522. Sampling part of task?

523. Who is responsible?

2.25 Quality Metrics: Services Offer

524. Was review conducted per standard protocols?

525. Which are the right metrics to use?

526. If the defect rate during testing is substantially higher than that of the previous release (or a similar product), then ask: Did you plan for and actually improve testing effectiveness?

527. How can the effectiveness of each of the activities be measured?

528. There are many reasons to shore up quality-related metrics, and what metrics are important?

529. Do you stratify metrics by product or site?

530. Was material distributed on time?

531. What is the timeline to meet your goal?

532. How should customers provide input?

533. Who notifies stakeholders of normal and abnormal results?

534. Why is now the time for quality metrics?

535. How effective are your security tests?

536. What documentation is required?

537. Are quality metrics defined?

538. Has trace of defects been initiated?

539. What happens if you get an abnormal result?

540. Filter visualizations of interest?

541. Are documents on hand to provide explanations of privacy and confidentiality?

542. What metrics do you measure?

2.26 Process Improvement Plan: Services Offer

543. Where do you want to be?

544. The motive is determined by asking, Why do you want to achieve this goal?

545. What personnel are the coaches for your initiative?

546. What makes people good SPI coaches?

547. What actions are needed to address the problems and achieve the goals?

548. What is the test-cycle concept?

549. Are you following the quality standards?

550. Are you making progress on the goals?

551. What lessons have you learned so far?

552. Has a process guide to collect the data been developed?

553. Are you making progress on your improvement plan?

554. What personnel are the champions for the initiative?

555. What is quality and how will you ensure it?

556. Why do you want to achieve the goal?

557. Everyone agrees on what process improvement is, right?

558. Have the frequency of collection and the points in the process where measurements will be made been determined?

559. Does your process ensure quality?

560. Are there forms and procedures to collect and record the data?

2.27 Responsibility Assignment Matrix: Services Offer

561. Incurrence of actual indirect costs in excess of budgets, by element of expense?

562. Are the actual costs used for variance analysis reconcilable with data from the accounting system?

563. Does the scheduling system identify in a timely manner the status of work?

564. Are management actions taken to reduce indirect costs when there are significant adverse variances?

565. Does a missing responsibility indicate that the current Services Offer project is not yet fully understood?

566. What are the known stakeholder requirements?

567. How do you assist them to be as productive as possible?

568. Does the accounting system provide a basis for auditing records of direct costs chargeable to the contract?

569. Are all elements of indirect expense identified to overhead cost budgets of Services Offer projections?

570. Undistributed budgets, if any?

571. Does the contractor use objective results, design reviews and tests to trace schedule performance?

572. Are all authorized tasks assigned to identified organizational elements?

573. Who is responsible for work and budgets for each wbs?

574. What is the justification?

575. Is work properly classified as measured effort, LOE, or apportioned effort and appropriately separated?

576. When performing is split among two or more roles, is the work clearly defined so that the efforts are coordinated and the communication is clear?

577. What travel needed?

578. Are control accounts opened and closed based on the start and completion of work contained therein?

579. Are others working on the right things?

2.28 Roles and Responsibilities: Services Offer

580. What should you do now to prepare yourself for a promotion, increased responsibilities or a different job?

581. Once the responsibilities are defined for the Services Offer project, have the deliverables, roles and responsibilities been clearly communicated to every participant?

582. How is your work-life balance?

583. What areas would you highlight for changes or improvements?

584. Are Services Offer project team roles and responsibilities identified and documented?

585. Was the expectation clearly communicated?

586. Does the team have access to and ability to use data analysis tools?

587. Are Services Offer project team roles and responsibilities identified and documented?

588. Who is responsible for each task?

589. What should you highlight for improvement?

590. Influence: what areas of organizational decision

making are you able to influence when you do not have authority to make the final decision?

591. Is the data complete?

592. Does your vision/mission support a culture of quality data?

593. Is there a training program in place for stakeholders covering expectations, roles and responsibilities and any addition knowledge others need to be good stakeholders?

594. Are your policies supportive of a culture of quality data?

595. What is working well within your organizations performance management system?

596. Authority: what areas/Services Offer projects in your work do you have the authority to decide upon and act on the already stated decisions?

597. Are governance roles and responsibilities documented?

598. Who is responsible for implementation activities and where will the functions, roles and responsibilities be defined?

2.29 Human Resource Management Plan: Services Offer

599. Are the schedule estimates reasonable given the Services Offer project?

600. How to convince employees that this is a necessary process?

601. Are staff skills known and available for each task?

602. Were the budget estimates reasonable?

603. What areas does the group agree are the biggest success on the Services Offer project?

604. Measurable - are the targets measurable?

605. Is Services Offer project work proceeding in accordance with the original Services Offer project schedule?

606. Is an industry recognized support tool(s) being used for Services Offer project scheduling & tracking?

607. How will the Services Offer project manage expectations & meet needs and requirements?

608. Are enough systems & user personnel assigned to the Services Offer project?

609. Is your organization certified as a supplier, wholesaler, regular dealer, or manufacturer of

corresponding products/supplies?

610. Are schedule deliverables actually delivered?

611. Does the schedule include Services Offer project management time and change request analysis time?

612. Is there an approved case?

613. Are Services Offer project team members involved in detailed estimating and scheduling?

614. Are Services Offer project leaders committed to this Services Offer project full time?

615. Has the budget been baselined?

616. Is your organization primarily focused on a specific industry?

2.30 Communications Management Plan: Services Offer

617. Do you prepare stakeholder engagement plans?

618. Are stakeholders internal or external?

619. Are there potential barriers between the team and the stakeholder?

620. Why is stakeholder engagement important?

621. How were corresponding initiatives successful?

622. Do you then often overlook a key stakeholder or stakeholder group?

623. Who needs to know and how much?

624. Who are the members of the governing body?

625. Do you ask; can you recommend others for you to talk with about this initiative?

626. What data is going to be required?

627. Which stakeholders are thought leaders, influences, or early adopters?

628. Who did you turn to if you had questions?

629. Who have you worked with in past, similar initiatives?

630. What approaches do you use?

631. Which stakeholders can influence others?

632. Which team member will work with each stakeholder?

633. Who will use or be affected by the result of a Services Offer project?

634. What to learn?

635. What steps can you take for a positive relationship?

636. Is the stakeholder role recognized by your organization?

2.31 Risk Management Plan: Services Offer

637. How would you suggest monitoring for risk transition indicators?

638. Can it be changed quickly?

639. Do the people have the right combinations of skills?

640. Market risk -will the new service or product be useful to your organization or marketable to others?

641. Are the metrics meaningful and useful?

642. What are the cost, schedule and resource impacts of avoiding the risk?

643. Is Services Offer project scope stable?

644. What does a risk management program do?

645. How is risk monitoring performed?

646. Have you worked with the customer in the past?

647. What can you do to minimize the impact if it does?

648. Mitigation -how can you avoid the risk?

649. What is the impact to the Services Offer project if

the item is not resolved in a timely fashion?

650. Minimize cost and financial risk?

651. Are there alternative opinions/solutions/ processes you should explore?

652. How can you fix it?

653. What other risks are created by choosing an avoidance strategy?

654. Who/what can assist?

655. Risk probability and impact: how will the probabilities and impacts of risk items be assessed?

656. Is the necessary data being captured and is it complete and accurate?

2.32 Risk Register: Services Offer

657. Why would you develop a risk register?

658. Are corrective measures implemented as planned?

659. What should you do when?

660. Are there any knock-on effects/impact on any of the other areas?

661. Which key risks have ineffective responses or outstanding improvement actions?

662. Risk categories: what are the main categories of risks that should be addressed on this Services Offer project?

663. Technology risk -is the Services Offer project technically feasible?

664. How could corresponding Risk affect the Services Offer project in terms of cost and schedule?

665. Who is accountable?

666. What evidence do you have to justify the likelihood score of the risk (audit, incident report, claim, complaints, inspection, internal review)?

667. How are risks graded?

668. People risk -are people with appropriate skills

available to help complete the Services Offer project?

669. What risks might negatively or positively affect achieving the Services Offer project objectives?

670. What are the major risks facing the Services Offer project?

671. What is a Risk?

672. Are implemented controls working as others should?

673. When would you develop a risk register?

674. When will it happen?

675. Are your objectives at risk?

2.33 Probability and Impact Assessment: Services Offer

676. Why has this particular mode of contracting been chosen?

677. What are the probabilities of chosen technologies being suitable for local conditions?

678. How do risks change during a Services Offer project life cycle?

679. Workarounds are determined during which step of risk management?

680. How are you working with risks?

681. Who should be notified of the occurrence of each of the risk indicators?

682. How would you assess the risk management process in the Services Offer project?

683. What is the experience (performance, attitude, business ethics, etc.) in the past with contractors?

684. How do you define a risk?

685. Monitoring of the overall Services Offer project status – are there any changes in the Services Offer project that can effect and cause new possible risks?

686. Are formal technical reviews part of this process?

687. Is the customer willing to establish rapid communication links with the developer?

688. Supply/demand Services Offer projections and trends; what are the levels of accuracy?

689. What is the likelihood of a breakthrough?

690. What should be done with non-critical risks?

691. What will be the likely political environment during the life of the Services Offer project?

692. Are the facilities, expertise, resources, and management know-how available to handle the situation?

693. What significant shift will occur in governmental policies, laws, and regulations pertaining to specific industries?

694. How do the products attain the specifications?

695. Has something like this been done before?

2.34 Probability and Impact Matrix: Services Offer

696. What are the methods to deal with risks?

697. What are the chances the risk events will occur?

698. What are data sources?

699. Degree of confidence in estimated size estimate?

700. Which should be probably done NEXT?

701. What will be the likely political situation during the life of the Services Offer project?

702. What lifestyle shifts might occur in society?

703. Are the risk data complete?

704. Do you have a consistent repeatable process that is actually used?

705. Are testing tools available and suitable?

706. Management -what contingency plans do you have if the risk becomes a reality?

707. How is the risk management process used in practice?

708. What are the probable external agencies to act as Services Offer project manager?

709. Is security a central objective?

710. Which is the BEST thing to do?

711. Are some people working on multiple Services Offer projects?

712. Could others have been better mitigated?

713. Who are the owners?

2.35 Risk Data Sheet: Services Offer

714. What can you do?

715. During work activities could hazards exist?

716. Has the most cost-effective solution been chosen?

717. What are your core values?

718. Potential for recurrence?

719. What do you know?

720. How do you handle product safely?

721. If it happens, what are the consequences?

722. Type of risk identified?

723. What is the likelihood of it happening?

724. What is the environment within which you operate (social trends, economic, community values, broad based participation, national directions etc.)?

725. Will revised controls lead to tolerable risk levels?

726. What do people affected think about the need for, and practicality of preventive measures?

727. What are you weak at and therefore need to do better?

728. What will be the consequences if the risk happens?

729. Has a sensitivity analysis been carried out?

730. How reliable is the data source?

731. What was measured?

2.36 Procurement Management Plan: Services Offer

732. Has the Services Offer project manager been identified?

733. Is the steering committee active in Services Offer project oversight?

734. What is the last item a Services Offer project manager must do to finalize Services Offer project close-out?

735. Services Offer project Objectives?

736. Are the Services Offer project team members located locally to the users/stakeholders?

737. Are milestone deliverables effectively tracked and compared to Services Offer project plan?

738. Were Services Offer project team members involved in the development of activity & task decomposition?

739. What were things that you did well, and could improve, and how?

740. What were things that you did very well and want to do the same again on the next Services Offer project?

741. Has the business need been clearly defined?

742. Is the current scope of the Services Offer project substantially different than that originally defined?

743. Are the quality tools and methods identified in the Quality Plan appropriate to the Services Offer project?

744. Are status reports received per the Services Offer project Plan?

745. Has a Services Offer project Communications Plan been developed?

746. How will multiple providers be managed?

747. Are Services Offer project team roles and responsibilities identified and documented?

2.37 Source Selection Criteria: Services Offer

748. Are evaluators ready to begin this task?

749. What is cost analysis and when should it be performed?

750. Is this a cost contract?

751. When is it appropriate to conduct a preproposal conference?

752. When is it appropriate to issue a DRFP?

753. How should the oral presentations be handled?

754. How should oral presentations be evaluated?

755. In order of importance, which evaluation criteria are the most critical to the determination of your overall rating?

756. What procedures are followed when a contractor requires access to classified information or a significant quantity of special material/information?

757. What will you use to capture evaluation and subsequent documentation?

758. How do you encourage efficiency and consistency?

759. Why promote competition?

760. How long will it take for the purchase cost to be the same as the lease cost?

761. Which contract type places the most risk on the seller?

762. How much weight should be placed on past performance information?

763. How organization are proposed quotes/prices?

764. What information is to be provided and when should it be provided?

765. What should be the contracting officers strategy?

766. Do you have a plan to document consensus results including disposition of any disagreement by individual evaluators?

767. When and what information can be considered with offerors regarding past performance?

2.38 Stakeholder Management Plan: Services Offer

768. Are action items captured and managed?

769. Has the schedule been baselined?

770. Are parking lot items captured?

771. Have all necessary approvals been obtained?

772. Is the quality assurance team identified?

773. Are Services Offer project contact logs kept up to date?

774. Are decisions captured in a decisions log?

775. Will the current technology alter during the life of the Services Offer project?

776. Does this include subcontracted development?

777. Have stakeholder accountabilities & responsibilities been clearly defined?

778. Has a Services Offer project Communications Plan been developed?

779. What inspection and testing is to be performed?

780. Have Services Offer project management standards and procedures been established and

documented?

781. Have the key elements of a coherent Services Offer project management strategy been established?

782. Are all resource assumptions documented?

783. What is the primary function of the Activity Decomposition Decision Tree?

784. Is there an onboarding process in place?

2.39 Change Management Plan: Services Offer

785. What new behaviours are required?

786. Is there a software application relevant to this deliverable?

787. Have the business unit contacts been selected and notified?

788. Will the culture embrace or reject this change?

789. What policies and procedures need to be changed?

790. What are the responsibilities assigned to each role?

791. Who might present the most resistance?

792. Why would a Services Offer project run more smoothly when change management is emphasized from the beginning?

793. Will all field readiness criteria have been practically met prior to training roll-out?

794. Why is the initiative is being undertaken - What are the business drivers?

795. Has the priority for this Services Offer project been set by the Business Unit Management Team?

796. Is there a need for new relationships to be built?

797. What are the major changes to processes?

798. Who might be able to help you the most?

799. Who will do the training?

800. Do you need new systems?

801. What are the current methods of sharing information and do there need to be new ones developed?

802. What risks may occur upfront?

803. Which relationships will change?

3.0 Executing Process Group: Services Offer

804. What are the main types of contracts if you do decide to outsource?

805. What type of information goes in the quality assurance plan?

806. What are the main processes included in Services Offer project quality management?

807. What are deliverables of your Services Offer project?

808. Are escalated issues resolved promptly?

809. Does the Services Offer project team have enough people to execute the Services Offer project plan?

810. Does the Services Offer project team have the right skills?

811. Who will provide training?

812. What is the difference between using brainstorming and the Delphi technique for risk identification?

813. When will the Services Offer project be done?

814. What are the typical Services Offer project

management skills?

815. How do you prevent staff are just doing busywork to pass the time?

816. How will you know you did it?

817. Does software appear easy to learn?

818. What areas does the group agree are the biggest success on the Services Offer project?

819. Do Services Offer project managers understand your organizational context for Services Offer projects?

820. Have operating capacities been created and/or reinforced in partners?

821. What are the key components of the Services Offer project communications plan?

822. What are deliverables of your Services Offer project?

3.1 Team Member Status Report: Services Offer

823. How does this product, good, or service meet the needs of the Services Offer project and your organization as a whole?

824. The problem with Reward & Recognition Programs is that the truly deserving people all too often get left out. How can you make it practical?

825. How can you make it practical?

826. Will the staff do training or is that done by a third party?

827. How it is to be done?

828. Why is it to be done?

829. What specific interest groups do you have in place?

830. What is to be done?

831. Is there evidence that staff is taking a more professional approach toward management of your organizations Services Offer projects?

832. Does your organization have the means (staff, money, contract, etc.) to produce or to acquire the product, good, or service?

833. Does every department have to have a Services Offer project Manager on staff?

834. How much risk is involved?

835. Does the product, good, or service already exist within your organization?

836. How will resource planning be done?

837. Are your organizations Services Offer projects more successful over time?

838. Are the attitudes of staff regarding Services Offer project work improving?

839. Are the products of your organizations Services Offer projects meeting customers objectives?

840. When a teams productivity and success depend on collaboration and the efficient flow of information, what generally fails them?

841. Do you have an Enterprise Services Offer project Management Office (EPMO)?

3.2 Change Request: Services Offer

842. What is the relationship between requirements attributes and attributes like complexity and size?

843. What mechanism is used to appraise others of changes that are made?

844. Which requirements attributes affect the risk to reliability the most?

845. Where do changes come from?

846. What are the duties of the change control team?

847. How are changes graded and who is responsible for the rating?

848. Why do you want to have a change control system?

849. How does a team identify the discrete elements of a configuration?

850. How does your organization control changes before and after software is released to a customer?

851. Should a more thorough impact analysis be conducted?

852. Has a formal technical review been conducted to assess technical correctness?

853. When to submit a change request?

854. What must be taken into consideration when introducing change control programs?

855. Will new change requests be acknowledged in a timely manner?

856. Who is responsible for the implementation and monitoring of all measures?

857. Will this change conflict with other requirements changes (e.g., lead to conflicting operational scenarios)?

858. How fast will change requests be approved?

859. Since there are no change requests in your Services Offer project at this point, what must you have before you begin?

860. Who can suggest changes?

3.3 Change Log: Services Offer

861. Is the change backward compatible without limitations?

862. Is the submitted change a new change or a modification of a previously approved change?

863. When was the request submitted?

864. Who initiated the change request?

865. Is the change request within Services Offer project scope?

866. How does this change affect the timeline of the schedule?

867. Does the suggested change request represent a desired enhancement to the products functionality?

868. How does this relate to the standards developed for specific business processes?

869. Is the requested change request a result of changes in other Services Offer project(s)?

870. Do the described changes impact on the integrity or security of the system?

871. Does the suggested change request seem to represent a necessary enhancement to the product?

872. Is this a mandatory replacement?

873. Will the Services Offer project fail if the change request is not executed?

874. Is the change request open, closed or pending?

875. When was the request approved?

876. How does this change affect scope?

3.4 Decision Log: Services Offer

877. Which variables make a critical difference?

878. Who will be given a copy of this document and where will it be kept?

879. Adversarial environment. is your opponent open to a non-traditional workflow, or will it likely challenge anything you do?

880. Meeting purpose; why does this team meet?

881. It becomes critical to track and periodically revisit both operational effectiveness; Are you noticing all that you need to, and are you interpreting what you see effectively?

882. What alternatives/risks were considered?

883. Decision-making process; how will the team make decisions?

884. With whom was the decision shared or considered?

885. How do you define success?

886. What is the line where eDiscovery ends and document review begins?

887. Who is the decisionmaker?

888. What are the cost implications?

889. Does anything need to be adjusted?

890. How does provision of information, both in terms of content and presentation, influence acceptance of alternative strategies?

891. What is your overall strategy for quality control / quality assurance procedures?

892. How do you know when you are achieving it?

893. At what point in time does loss become unacceptable?

894. Behaviors; what are guidelines that the team has identified that will assist them with getting the most out of team meetings?

895. What is the average size of your matters in an applicable measurement?

896. Is your opponent open to a non-traditional workflow, or will it likely challenge anything you do?

3.5 Quality Audit: Services Offer

897. What does an analysis of your organizations staff profile suggest in terms of its planning, and how is this being addressed?

898. How does your organization know that its staff financial services are appropriately effective and constructive?

899. Is progress against the intentions measurable?

900. How does your organization know that its management system is appropriately effective and constructive?

901. How does the organization know that its system for maintaining and advancing the capabilities of its staff, particularly in relation to the Mission of the organization, is appropriately effective and constructive?

902. How are you auditing your organizations compliance with regulations?

903. Can your organization demonstrate exactly how and why results were achieved?

904. How does your organization know that its system for staff performance planning and review is appropriately effective and constructive?

905. How does your organization know that its systems for communicating with and among staff are

appropriately effective and constructive?

906. How does your organization know that its systems for providing high quality consultancy services to external parties are appropriately effective and constructive?

907. How does your organization know that its system for commercializing research outputs is appropriately effective and constructive?

908. How does your organization know that its system for attending to the health and wellbeing of its staff is appropriately effective and constructive?

909. Are the review comments incorporated?

910. What is the collective experience of the team to be assigned to an audit?

911. How does your organization know that its quality of teaching is appropriately effective and constructive?

912. How does your organization know that the quality of its supervisors is appropriately effective and constructive?

913. Does the supplier use a formal quality system?

914. Statements of intent remain exactly that until they are put into effect. The next step is to deploy the already stated intentions. In other words, do the plans happen in reality?

915. How does your organization know that the

system for managing its facilities is appropriately effective and constructive?

916. What mechanisms exist for identification of staff development needs?

3.6 Team Directory: Services Offer

917. Process decisions: do invoice amounts match accepted work in place?

918. When does information need to be distributed?

919. When will you produce deliverables?

920. Who will write the meeting minutes and distribute?

921. Decisions: what could be done better to improve the quality of the constructed product?

922. Process decisions: how well was task order work performed?

923. Does a Services Offer project team directory list all resources assigned to the Services Offer project?

924. Process decisions: do job conditions warrant additional actions to collect job information and document on-site activity?

925. Who should receive information (all stakeholders)?

926. Who will be the stakeholders on your next Services Offer project?

927. Who will report Services Offer project status to all stakeholders?

928. Days from the time the issue is identified?

929. How will you accomplish and manage the objectives?

930. What needs to be communicated?

931. Why is the work necessary?

932. What are you going to deliver or accomplish?

933. How do unidentified risks impact the outcome of the Services Offer project?

934. Contract requirements complied with?

3.7 Team Operating Agreement: Services Offer

935. How will your group handle planned absences?

936. What are some potential sources of conflict among team members?

937. What types of accommodations will be formulated and put in place for sustaining the team?

938. The method to be used in the decision making process; Will it be consensus, majority rule, or the supervisor having the final say?

939. What are the current caseload numbers in the unit?

940. Do you call or email participants to ensure understanding, follow-through and commitment to the meeting outcomes?

941. Do you post any action items, due dates, and responsibilities on the team website?

942. Do you upload presentation materials in advance and test the technology?

943. Are there the right people on your team?

944. Do you begin with a question to engage everyone?

945. How do you want to be thought of and known within your organization?

946. Did you recap the meeting purpose, time, and expectations?

947. What is culture?

948. What are the boundaries (organizational or geographic) within which you operate?

949. To whom do you deliver your services?

950. Do you vary your voice pace, tone and pitch to engage participants and gain involvement?

951. Methodologies: how will key team processes be implemented, such as training, research, work deliverable production, review and approval processes, knowledge management, and meeting procedures?

952. Are there more than two functional areas represented by your team?

953. What is the number of cases currently teamed?

954. How does teaming fit in with overall organizational goals and meet organizational needs?

3.8 Team Performance Assessment: Services Offer

955. Do friends perform better than acquaintances?

956. To what degree do team members articulate the teams work approach?

957. When a reviewer complains about method variance, what is the essence of the complaint?

958. How much interpersonal friction is there in your team?

959. To what degree do members articulate the goals beyond the team membership?

960. What are teams?

961. To what degree do all members feel responsible for all agreed-upon measures?

962. To what degree does the teams purpose contain themes that are particularly meaningful and memorable?

963. To what degree does the teams work approach provide opportunity for members to engage in fact-based problem solving?

964. Do you give group members authority to make at least some important decisions?

965. If you have criticized someones work for method variance in your role as reviewer, what was the circumstance?

966. To what degree are corresponding categories of skills either actually or potentially represented across the membership?

967. To what degree will the approach capitalize on and enhance the skills of all team members in a manner that takes into consideration other demands on members of the team?

968. To what degree do team members feel that the purpose of the team is important, if not exciting?

969. To what degree are staff involved as partners in the improvement process?

970. Is there a particular method of data analysis that you would recommend as a means of demonstrating that method variance is not of great concern for a given dataset?

971. To what degree do members understand and articulate the same purpose without relying on ambiguous abstractions?

972. How do you manage human resources?

973. To what degree can team members vigorously define the teams purpose in considerations with others who are not part of the functioning team?

974. How hard do you try to make a good selection?

3.9 Team Member Performance Assessment: Services Offer

975. How are evaluation results utilized?

976. What makes them effective?

977. What specific plans do you have for developing effective cross-platform assessments in a blended learning environment?

978. What are top priorities?

979. To what degree are the goals ambitious?

980. To what degree does the team possess adequate membership to achieve its ends?

981. Who receives a benchmark visit?

982. How often should assessments be conducted?

983. To what degree can all members engage in open and interactive considerations?

984. How do you work together to improve teaching and learning?

985. What is the role of the Reviewer?

986. What evaluation results did you have?

987. How is your organizations Strategic Management

System tied to performance measurement?

988. How do you make use of research?

989. What is the Business Management Oversight Process?

990. For what period of time is a member rated?

991. Is there reluctance to join a team?

992. What is the large, desired outcome?

993. What innovations (if any) are developed to realize goals?

994. How is performance assessment used in making future award decisions including options and extend/compete decisions?

3.10 Issue Log: Services Offer

995. How often do you engage with stakeholders?

996. Why do you manage communications?

997. What is the status of the issue?

998. Who is the issue assigned to?

999. What would have to change?

1000. What are the stakeholders interrelationships?

1001. Is the issue log kept in a safe place?

1002. What does the stakeholder need from the team?

1003. Who do you turn to if you have questions?

1004. Do you feel a register helps?

1005. Who were proponents/opponents?

1006. How do you manage communications?

1007. Can you think of other people who might have concerns or interests?

1008. Why do you manage human resources?

4.0 Monitoring and Controlling Process Group: Services Offer

1009. Where is the Risk in the Services Offer project?

1010. Were sponsors and decision makers available when needed outside regularly scheduled meetings?

1011. How to ensure validity, quality and consistency?

1012. What are the goals of the program?

1013. Are there areas that need improvement?

1014. Were escalated issues resolved promptly?

1015. What is the timeline for the Services Offer project?

1016. How well defined and documented were the Services Offer project management processes you chose to use?

1017. Feasibility: how much money, time, and effort can you put into this?

1018. Is it what was agreed upon?

1019. If action is called for, what form should it take?

1020. User: who wants the information and what are they interested in?

1021. Contingency planning. if a risk event occurs, what will you do?

1022. Who needs to be involved in the planning?

1023. How well did the chosen processes fit the needs of the Services Offer project?

1024. How was the program set-up initiated?

1025. How will staff learn how to use the deliverables?

4.1 Project Performance Report: Services Offer

1026. To what degree does the teams work approach provide opportunity for members to engage in results-based evaluation?

1027. To what degree does the task meet individual needs?

1028. To what degree does the funding match the requirement?

1029. To what degree are the demands of the task compatible with and converge with the mission and functions of the formal organization?

1030. To what degree does the informal organization make use of individual resources and meet individual needs?

1031. To what degree can team members frequently and easily communicate with one another?

1032. To what degree is the information network consistent with the structure of the formal organization?

1033. To what degree can the team ensure that all members are individually and jointly accountable for the teams purpose, goals, approach, and work-products?

1034. To what degree is the team cognizant of small wins to be celebrated along the way?

1035. What degree are the relative importance and priority of the goals clear to all team members?

1036. To what degree does the formal organization make use of individual resources and meet individual needs?

1037. To what degree are sub-teams possible or necessary?

1038. To what degree are the structures of the formal organization consistent with the behaviors in the informal organization?

1039. To what degree can the cognitive capacity of individuals accommodate the flow of information?

1040. To what degree do team members agree with the goals, relative importance, and the ways in which achievement will be measured?

1041. What is in it for you?

1042. To what degree are the teams goals and objectives clear, simple, and measurable?

4.2 Variance Analysis: Services Offer

1043. Is the entire contract planned in time-phased control accounts to the extent practicable?

1044. What costs are avoidable if one or more customers are dropped?

1045. When, during the last four quarters, did a primary business event occur causing a fluctuation?

1046. Are there quarterly budgets with quarterly performance comparisons?

1047. Other relevant issues of Variance Analysis -selling price or gross margin?

1048. Do work packages consist of discrete tasks which are adequately described?

1049. Are records maintained to show how undistributed budgets are controlled?

1050. What is the incurrence of actual indirect costs in excess of budgets, by element of expense?

1051. What is the total budget for the Services Offer project (including estimates for authorized and unpriced work)?

1052. What business event causes fluctuations?

1053. Do the rates and prices remain constant throughout the year?

1054. Are meaningful indicators identified for use in measuring the status of cost and schedule performance?

1055. Are the requirements for all items of overhead established by rational, traceable processes?

1056. Did an existing competitor change strategy?

1057. Are there changes in the direct base to which overhead costs are allocated?

1058. Are the wbs and organizational levels for application of the Services Offer projected overhead costs identified?

1059. Can the contractor substantiate work package and planning package budgets?

1060. Is there a logical explanation for any variance?

1061. What is the expected future profitability of each customer?

4.3 Earned Value Status: Services Offer

1062. Are you hitting your Services Offer projects targets?

1063. Validation is a process of ensuring that the developed system will actually achieve the stakeholders desired outcomes; Are you building the right product? What do you validate?

1064. When is it going to finish?

1065. What is the unit of forecast value?

1066. Where are your problem areas?

1067. Earned value can be used in almost any Services Offer project situation and in almost any Services Offer project environment. it may be used on large Services Offer projects, medium sized Services Offer projects, tiny Services Offer projects (in cut-down form), complex and simple Services Offer projects and in any market sector. some people, of course, know all about earned value, they have used it for years - but perhaps not as effectively as they could have?

1068. Where is evidence-based earned value in your organization reported?

1069. Verification is a process of ensuring that the developed system satisfies the stakeholders agreements and specifications; Are you building the product right? What do you verify?

1070. How does this compare with other Services Offer projects?

1071. How much is it going to cost by the finish?

1072. If earned value management (EVM) is so good in determining the true status of a Services Offer project and Services Offer project its completion, why is it that hardly any one uses it in information systems related Services Offer projects?

4.4 Risk Audit: Services Offer

1073. Does the implementation method matter?

1074. What are the outcomes you are looking for?

1075. Does your organization have or has considered the need for insurance covers: public liability, professional indemnity and directors and officers liability?

1076. Estimated size of product in number of programs, files, transactions?

1077. Are you willing to seek legal advice when required?

1078. Do you manage the process through use of metrics?

1079. What limitations do auditors face in effectively applying risk-assessment results to the risk of material misstatement measures?

1080. Which assets are important?

1081. What expertise do auditors need to generate effective business-level risk assessments, and to what extent do auditors currently possess the already stated attributes?

1082. Does the adoption of a business risk audit approach change internal control documentation and testing practices?

1083. Is a software Services Offer project management tool available?

1084. What is the implication of budget constraint on this process?

1085. Are end-users enthusiastically committed to the Services Offer project and the system/product to be built?

1086. Can analytical tests provide evidence that is as strong as evidence from traditional substantive tests?

1087. Is the customer willing to participate in reviews?

1088. Are audit program plans risk-adjusted?

1089. Does your board meet regularly and document all decisions and actions?

1090. Are duties out-of-class?

1091. Is Services Offer project scope stable?

4.5 Contractor Status Report: Services Offer

1092. What was the overall budget or estimated cost?

1093. What was the budget or estimated cost for your organizations services?

1094. What was the actual budget or estimated cost for your organizations services?

1095. What process manages the contracts?

1096. What is the average response time for answering a support call?

1097. Who can list a Services Offer project as organization experience, your organization or a previous employee of your organization?

1098. Are there contractual transfer concerns?

1099. Describe how often regular updates are made to the proposed solution. Are corresponding regular updates included in the standard maintenance plan?

1100. How is risk transferred?

1101. If applicable; describe your standard schedule for new software version releases. Are new software version releases included in the standard maintenance plan?

1102. How does the proposed individual meet each requirement?

1103. How long have you been using the services?

1104. What was the final actual cost?

1105. What are the minimum and optimal bandwidth requirements for the proposed solution?

4.6 Formal Acceptance: Services Offer

1106. What function(s) does it fill or meet?

1107. Was the Services Offer project goal achieved?

1108. Who supplies data?

1109. What can you do better next time?

1110. What is the Acceptance Management Process?

1111. Have all comments been addressed?

1112. Is formal acceptance of the Services Offer project product documented and distributed?

1113. How well did the team follow the methodology?

1114. Do you perform formal acceptance or burn-in tests?

1115. Was the client satisfied with the Services Offer project results?

1116. Did the Services Offer project manager and team act in a professional and ethical manner?

1117. Do you buy-in installation services?

1118. Was the Services Offer project work done on time, within budget, and according to specification?

1119. Who would use it?

1120. Did the Services Offer project achieve its MOV?

1121. Does it do what Services Offer project team said it would?

1122. Do you buy pre-configured systems or build your own configuration?

1123. What features, practices, and processes proved to be strengths or weaknesses?

1124. What are the requirements against which to test, Who will execute?

1125. General estimate of the costs and times to complete the Services Offer project?

5.0 Closing Process Group: Services Offer

1126. How well did the chosen processes fit the needs of the Services Offer project?

1127. What could be done to improve the process?

1128. Just how important is your work to the overall success of the Services Offer project?

1129. What areas were overlooked on this Services Offer project?

1130. Did the delivered product meet the specified requirements and goals of the Services Offer project?

1131. Was the schedule met?

1132. Was the user/client satisfied with the end product?

1133. Were risks identified and mitigated?

1134. What can you do better next time, and what specific actions can you take to improve?

1135. Is this a follow-on to a previous Services Offer project?

1136. How critical is the Services Offer project success to the success of your organization?

1137. Are there funding or time constraints?

1138. What could have been improved?

1139. What level of risk does the proposed budget represent to the Services Offer project?

1140. Based on your Services Offer project communication management plan, what worked well?

5.1 Procurement Audit: Services Offer

1141. Are there procedures for trade-in arrangements?

1142. Are there appropriate controls in place to ensure that the procurement Services Offer project complies with relevant legislation?

1143. Are there mechanisms for evaluating the departments suppliers performance in relation to prices, quality, delivery and innovation?

1144. Was invitation to tender to each specific contract issued after the evaluation of the indicative tenders was completed?

1145. Are travel expenditures monitored to determine that they are in line with other employees and reasonable for the area of travel?

1146. Is there management monitoring of transactions and balances?

1147. Does your organization make sources of information beyond the tender documents equally available for all the candidates?

1148. Were all interested operators allowed the opportunity to participate?

1149. Did the contracting authority verify compliance with the basic requirements of the competition?

1150. Does the individual approving disbursements sign or initial the document?

1151. Is the purchasing department responsible for a continual review of marketing trends, particularly on long-term contracts and contracts containing escalation clauses?

1152. Are unsuccessful companies informed why tender failed?

1153. Are all checks stored in a secure area?

1154. Are there internal control systems in place to secure that laws and regulations are observed?

1155. Are all pre-numbered checks accounted for on a regular basis?

1156. Does your organization use existing contracts where possible to avoid the cost of bidding?

1157. Are unusual uses of organization funds investigated?

1158. Were exclusion causes duly considered before the actual evaluation of tenders?

1159. When performance conditions were detailed in the tender documentation, did the contracting authority verify if the tenders received met the already stated requirements?

1160. Was the expert likely to gain privileged knowledge from his activity which could be advantageous for him in a subsequent competition?

5.2 Contract Close-Out: Services Offer

1161. Parties: who is involved?

1162. How is the contracting office notified of the automatic contract close-out?

1163. Change in circumstances?

1164. Change in attitude or behavior?

1165. Have all contracts been completed?

1166. Has each contract been audited to verify acceptance and delivery?

1167. Parties: Authorized?

1168. How does it work?

1169. What is capture management?

1170. How/when used ?

1171. What happens to the recipient of services?

1172. Have all contract records been included in the Services Offer project archives?

1173. Have all acceptance criteria been met prior to final payment to contractors?

1174. Are the signers the authorized officials?

1175. Change in knowledge?

1176. Was the contract complete without requiring numerous changes and revisions?

1177. Was the contract sufficiently clear so as not to result in numerous disputes and misunderstandings?

1178. Have all contracts been closed?

1179. Was the contract type appropriate?

5.3 Project or Phase Close-Out: Services Offer

1180. How much influence did the stakeholder have over others?

1181. Who controlled key decisions that were made?

1182. What are the informational communication needs for each stakeholder?

1183. Did the Services Offer project management methodology work?

1184. What hierarchical authority does the stakeholder have in your organization?

1185. In addition to assessing whether the Services Offer project was successful, it is equally critical to analyze why it was or was not fully successful. Are you including this?

1186. What were the desired outcomes?

1187. What benefits or impacts does the stakeholder group expect to obtain as a result of the Services Offer project?

1188. Were cost budgets met?

1189. What information did each stakeholder need to contribute to the Services Offer projects success?

1190. Complete yes or no?

1191. Planned remaining costs?

1192. Who is responsible for award close-out?

1193. Does the lesson describe a function that would be done differently the next time?

1194. Did the delivered product meet the specified requirements and goals of the Services Offer project?

1195. Who are the Services Offer project stakeholders and what are roles and involvement?

1196. If you were the Services Offer project sponsor, how would you determine which Services Offer project team(s) and/or individuals deserve recognition?

1197. What was the preferred delivery mechanism?

5.4 Lessons Learned: Services Offer

1198. Can the lesson learned be replicated?

1199. How effective were your functional specs?

1200. Is the lesson significant, valid, and applicable?

1201. What are the funding priorities for intelligence?

1202. What is the growth stage of your organization?

1203. What are the influence patterns?

1204. What was helpful to know when planning the deployment?

1205. How well is the build process working?

1206. For the next Services Offer project, how could you improve on the way Services Offer project was conducted?

1207. What were the challenges and pitfalls?

1208. What surprises did the team have to deal with?

1209. What other questions should you have asked?

1210. Would you spend your own money to fix this issue?

1211. What skills are required for the task?

1212. Was the Services Offer project manager sufficiently experienced, skilled, trained, supported?

1213. Do you conduct the engineering tests?

1214. Was the purpose of the Services Offer project, the end products and success criteria clearly defined and agreed at the start?

1215. What would you like to see better documented about how to use existing processes on this type of Services Offer project?

1216. How actively and meaningfully were stakeholders involved in the Services Offer project?

Index

broken 68
broker 171
budget		94, 97, 114, 133-134, 154, 172, 189-190, 237, 242-243, 245, 248
budgeted	45
budgeting	150
budgets		18, 121, 150-151, 185-186, 237-238, 253
building		23, 97, 128, 164, 239
burn-in 245
business		1, 7, 11, 18, 36, 41, 45, 47, 62, 75, 79, 94, 103, 108, 110-111, 115-117, 121-122, 138, 140, 197, 203, 209, 217, 231, 237, 241
busywork		125, 212
button 11
buy-in 114, 245
Calculate		158, 160, 166
called 233
candidates	249
cannot160, 174
capability	18, 128, 178
capable		7, 39
capacities	122, 212
capacity		18, 23, 85, 128, 236
capital 104
capitalize	59, 229
capture		98, 205, 251
captured		53, 62, 79, 136, 194, 207
career 142
careers		104
carried 71, 202
caseload		226
catalog		118
categories	195, 229
caused		1
causes 45-46, 48, 58, 64, 72, 98, 132, 151, 237, 250
causing		22, 147, 237
celebrate	80
celebrated	236
center 134
central 200
centrally		84
centre 117
certain 126

duties 215, 242
dynamics   40
earlier 118
earned   5, 239-240
easily 235
economic   201
economical   120
Economy   86, 130
eDiscovery   219
edition 9
editorial   1
education   25, 93
effect 197, 222
effective   22-23, 103, 109, 146, 181, 221-223, 230, 241, 255
effects 48, 150, 158, 195
efficiency   66, 94, 205
efficient   46, 85, 214
effort   46, 50, 117, 134, 150, 186, 233
efforts 37, 86, 137, 186
either   229
electronic   1
element   185, 237
elements   11-12, 36, 65, 90, 118, 145, 151, 185-186, 208, 215
embarking   40
embrace   209
emerging   59, 100
emphasized   209
employee   78, 120, 243
employees   19, 22, 24, 70, 80, 103, 123, 179, 189, 249
employers   129
empower   7
enable 62
enablers   105
encourage   80, 96, 205
end-users   242
engage   114, 226-228, 230, 232, 235
engagement 129, 191
enhance   97, 229
enhanced   104
enough   7, 66, 111, 141, 143, 171, 189, 211
ensure 33, 39, 65, 69, 102, 109, 111, 113, 122, 146-147, 184, 226, 233, 235, 249
ensures   111

guidance   1
guidelines   220
handle 162, 198, 201, 226
handled   139, 180, 205
happen   21, 196, 222
happening   111, 201
happens   7, 11, 31, 54, 111, 120, 137, 140, 174-175, 182,
201-202, 251
hardly 240
havent 119
having 226
hazards   201
health 222
hearing   108
helpdesk   117
helpful 255
helping   7, 127
hidden 47
higher 181
highest 24
high-level   35
highlight   187
Highly 60
high-tech   120
hijacking   121
hiring 97
historical   176
history 163, 177
hitters 60
hitting 239
honest 112
horizontal   130
housed   139
humans   7
hypotheses   58
identified   1, 18-19, 25, 27, 34, 39, 60, 66-67, 75, 81, 137, 146,
151-152, 156, 172, 177, 185-187, 201, 203-204, 207, 220, 225, 238,
247
identify 12, 21, 26, 59, 62, 65, 75, 150, 158, 175, 185, 215
ignore 27
ignoring   105
imbedded   98

impact 4, 38, 45, 47, 50, 52-53, 125, 177, 193-195, 197, 199, 215, 217, 225
impacted   53, 137
impacts   52, 137, 167, 193-194, 253
implement   23, 46, 65, 89
implicit 104
importance   205, 236
important   27, 31, 63, 67, 69, 104, 107-108, 111, 113, 115, 127, 133, 139, 163, 181, 191, 228-229, 241, 247
improve   2, 11-12, 74-76, 78, 80-84, 86-87, 125, 127, 163, 181, 203, 224, 230, 247, 255
improved   85-86, 88, 94, 248
improving   80, 214
inaccurate   138
incentives   98
incident   195
include   18, 75, 77, 139, 152, 190, 207
included   2, 9, 23, 55, 140, 167, 176, 211, 243, 251
INCLUDES   10
including   18, 29, 38, 41, 51, 56, 66, 90, 97, 99, 206, 231, 237, 253
incomplete   138
increase   75, 112
increased   106, 187
increasing   122
incurred   52
incurrence   185, 237
incurring   150
indemnity   241
in-depth   9, 12
indicate   68, 99, 109, 185
indicated   98
indicative   249
indicators   27, 54, 56, 63, 69, 81, 97, 193, 197, 238
indirect   56, 150-151, 185, 237
indirectly   1
individual   1, 48, 154, 169, 206, 235-236, 244, 250
industries   198
industry   99, 121, 189-190
infinite 111
influence   76, 114, 129, 187-188, 192, 220, 253, 255
influences   191
informal   235-236

involved   20, 23, 33, 49, 61, 67, 70, 82, 108, 125, 133, 137,
179, 190, 203, 214, 229, 234, 251, 256
involves   95, 138
issued 249
issues 19, 21-24, 27, 126, 128, 141, 145, 147, 162, 211, 233, 237
iteration   172
itself   1, 24
jointly 235
judgment   1
justified96
justify 195
killer   112
knock-on   195
know-how   198
knowledge   11, 32, 36-37, 59, 75, 88, 91, 93, 96-98, 119, 121,
178, 188, 227, 250, 252
lacked 98
largely 64
latest   9, 151
laundry   139
leader 22, 69, 81
leaders29, 61, 67, 94, 106, 118, 152, 179, 190-191
leadership   21, 32, 40, 86, 118, 130
learned   6, 98, 183, 255
learning   90, 96-97, 230
lesson 254-255
lessons 6, 77, 98, 183, 255
Leveling   156
levels   18, 24, 34, 63, 69, 81, 93, 99, 151, 198, 201, 238
leverage   34, 86, 98, 120, 167, 176
leveraged   37
liability 1, 241
licensed   1
lifecycle   50, 58
lifecycles   75
lifestyle 199
Lifetime   10
likelihood   84, 87, 195, 198, 201
likely   88, 94, 166, 178, 198-199, 219-220, 250
limitation   45
limited 11
linked 32
listed   1

originally 137, 204
originate 100
others 125, 139, 170, 175-176, 186, 188, 191-193, 196, 200, 215, 229, 253
otherwise 1, 177
outcome 13, 79, 225, 231
outcomes 87, 108, 176, 226, 239, 241, 253
outlined 95
output 34, 59, 61-62, 64-65, 67, 71, 99-100
outputs 32, 62, 64, 68, 71, 94, 162, 165-166, 222
outside 80, 126, 165, 233
outsource 68, 128, 211
outweigh 46
overall 12-13, 26, 48, 99, 103, 161, 169, 197, 205, 220, 227, 243, 247
overcome 176
overhead 151, 185, 238
overlook 191
overlooked 247
overruns 150
oversight 65, 136, 203, 231
overtime 153
owners 148, 200
ownership 41, 91
package 238
packages 150-151, 237
paradigms 119
paragraph 123
parallel 160
parameters 95
Pareto 60, 153
parking 207
particular 65, 197, 229
parties 75, 222, 251
partners 20, 33, 75, 92, 118, 158, 212, 229
pattern 157
patterns 85, 255
payment 251
pending 218
people 7, 19, 47, 53, 59, 72, 82, 93, 96, 102, 104, 112-113, 117-118, 120, 147, 165, 172, 183, 193, 195, 200-201, 211, 213, 226, 232, 239
perceive 110

processes   48, 59-60, 62, 65-68, 70, 72, 90, 94, 97, 125, 133, 146-147, 194, 210-211, 217, 227, 233-234, 238, 246-247, 256
produce   61, 125, 162, 174, 213, 224
produced   65, 87
produces   156
producing   142
product   1, 11, 63, 69, 104, 112, 119, 138, 144, 169, 181, 193, 201, 213-214, 217, 224, 239-242, 245, 247, 254
production   34, 106, 227
productive   185
products   1, 19-20, 53, 80, 111, 117-118, 127, 132-133, 142, 171, 190, 198, 214, 217, 256
profile 221
program   21, 56, 73, 97, 132-133, 136, 180, 188, 193, 233-234, 242
programs   134, 213, 216, 241
progress   42, 86, 99, 103, 106, 125, 132-133, 175, 183, 221
prohibited   151
project 2-7, 9, 19, 22, 26, 36, 54, 58, 63, 67, 80, 89, 95, 97, 103, 105, 107-108, 110, 112-113, 119, 124-129, 131-134, 136-139, 142, 144-149, 152-161, 163, 165-179, 185, 187, 189-190, 192-193, 195-199, 203-204, 207-209, 211-214, 216-218, 224-225, 233-235, 237, 239-240, 242-243, 245-249, 251, 253-256
projected   238
projects   2, 53, 115, 118, 124, 132-134, 142, 149, 153, 165, 177, 188, 200, 212-214, 239-240, 253
promising   112
promote   53, 59, 206
promotion   187
promptly   211, 233
proper 95, 139
properly   11, 29, 38, 125-126, 150, 186
proponents   232
proposal   159
proposals   100
proposed   23, 47, 50, 139, 206, 243-244, 248
protect   71
protected   62
protection   116
protocols   181
proved 246
provide   21, 61, 109, 113, 119, 129, 140-141, 150-151, 161, 173, 176, 181-182, 185, 211, 228, 235, 242

provided   8, 13, 95, 165, 172, 206
provider   99
providers   75, 204
provides   163
providing   95, 129, 159, 170, 222
provision   220
provisions   123
public 241
Published   172
publisher   1
pulled 118
purchase   9, 11, 206
purchased   11
purchasing   250
purpose   2, 11, 120, 163, 175, 219, 227-229, 235, 256
pushing   111
qualified   39, 60-61, 67, 69, 172
qualifies   66, 71
qualify 52, 61, 69
qualities   23
quality 1, 4-5, 11, 25, 47, 49, 51, 64-65, 70, 81, 92, 98, 110-111,
126, 132, 152-153, 165, 172, 179, 181-184, 188, 204, 207, 211, 220-
222, 224, 233, 249
quantified   100
quantify   52
quantity   205
quarterly   237
quarters   237
question   12-13, 17, 29, 44, 58, 74, 89, 102, 113, 226
questions   7, 9, 12, 68, 139, 165, 167, 191, 232, 255
quickly 12, 61, 65, 69, 193
quotes 206
radically   62
rather 121
rating 205, 215
rational   238
reached   25
reactivate   102
readiness   34, 209
readings   90
realistic   25, 69, 121, 134
reality 199, 222
realize 55, 231

respective   132
respond   132
responded   13
response   18, 21, 97-99, 243
responses   82, 195
responsive   167, 176
result   60, 87, 174-175, 182, 192, 217, 252-253
resulted   99
resulting   70, 145
results   9, 37, 39, 63, 74-75, 77-78, 80, 82, 85, 87, 95, 97, 125, 132-133, 157, 166, 175, 179, 181, 186, 206, 221, 230, 241, 245
Retain 102
retained   68
retention   46
retrospect   118
return   87, 106, 160, 179
revenue   24, 55
revenues   54
review 11-12, 34, 61, 134, 169, 177, 181, 195, 215, 219, 221-222, 227, 250
reviewed   31, 125, 144, 152, 166
reviewer   228-230
reviews11, 144, 146, 161, 171, 186, 197, 242
revised 59, 99, 151, 201
revisions   252
revisit   219
reward 48, 53, 213
rewarded   24
rewards   98
rework 44
rights   1
robustness   131
roll-out 209
routine 96, 151
safely   201
safety   111
sample165
samples   179
Sampling   153, 180
satisfied   245, 247
satisfies239
satisfying   114
savings30, 55, 59

solving 228
Someone   7
someones   229
something   106, 198
Sometimes   54
source 5, 105-106, 147, 202, 205
sources   35, 60, 64, 140, 166, 199, 226, 249
special 32, 95, 128, 205
specific   9, 24, 31, 37, 59, 110, 146, 155-157, 161-163, 165,
169, 173-174, 178, 190, 198, 213, 217, 230, 247, 249
specified   151, 247, 254
spoken 119
sponsor   27, 127, 172, 254
sponsors   20, 233
spread 99
stable   193, 242
staffed 42
staffing 18, 97, 134
standard   7, 91, 99, 162, 181, 243
standards   1, 11-12, 92, 94, 100, 126, 179, 183, 207, 217
started 9, 159-160
starting 12, 133
stated   111, 122, 151, 165, 188, 222, 241, 250
statement   3, 12, 79, 85, 127, 137, 144, 146, 174, 177
statements   13, 28, 37, 41, 43, 57-58, 73, 88, 100, 123, 222
status   5-6, 59, 125, 138, 152-153, 185, 197, 204, 213, 224, 232,
238-240, 243
statutory   171
steady 45
steering   136, 152, 203
stored   139, 250
strategic   55, 87, 99, 108, 171, 180, 230
strategies   86, 100, 106, 122, 132, 220
strategy   26, 41, 49, 55, 74, 76, 81, 97, 103, 119, 122-123,
130, 133, 146, 194, 206, 208, 220, 238
stratify 181
Stream 67, 72
strengths   147, 246
stretch 117
strict   72
strive   117
strong   242
Strongly   12, 17, 29, 44, 58, 74, 89, 102

understood   76-77, 185
undertake   62
undertaken   209
underway   77
uninformed   121
unique 115, 131, 177
Unless 7
unpriced   237
unresolved   139, 162
unusual   250
updated   9-10, 59, 144, 153, 161
updates   10, 98, 166, 243
upfront210
upload226
usability   84
useful 83, 92, 193
usefully 12, 26
utility   167
utilized 230
validate   52, 239
validated   31, 35, 59, 64, 125
Validation   239
validity 140, 233
valuable   7
values 94, 118, 150, 201
variables   100, 219
variance   5, 185, 228-229, 237-238
variances   136-137, 150-151, 172, 185
variation   17, 39, 60, 64, 100
vendor 77, 104, 126, 161, 171
vendors   19, 61, 75, 145
verified 10, 31, 35, 64, 125, 136, 158
verify 46-47, 49-56, 93-94, 96, 132, 145, 240, 249-251
verifying   46-47, 49
Version 243, 257
versions   30, 42
vertical 130
vertically   152
vested 116
vetting 147
viable 93, 148
vigorously   229
vision 118, 188

CPSIA information can be obtained
at www.ICGtesting.com
Printed in the USA
BVHW091513310719
554799BV00012B/595/P